BASIC
for
Business

BASIC for Business

Douglas Hergert

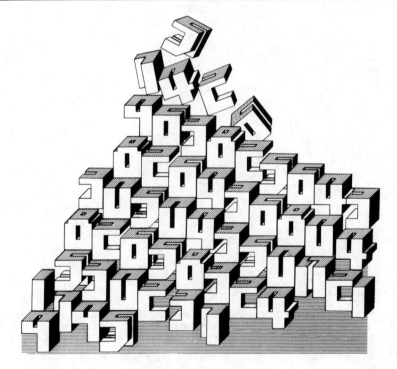

Berkeley • Paris • Düsseldorf

CREDITS
Cover illustration by Daniel Le Noury
Layout and technical illustrations by Jeanne E. Tennant

Apple II is a registered trademark of Apple Computer, Inc.
TRS-80 is a registered trademark of Tandy Corporation.
SYBEX is not affiliated with any manufacturer.

Library of Congress Card Number: 81-85955
ISBN 0-89588-080-6
First Edition 1982
Printed in the United States of America
10 9 8 7 6 5 4 3

To Elaine M. Andersson

Table of Contents

Acknowledgements

Several people contributed significantly to this book by reading the manuscript and making thoughtful suggestions. These include James Compton, whose editorial sense of style and clarity exerted a positive influence throughout this book; Mark Evanoff, Richard Hergert, Rudolph Langer, and X.T. Bui, who carefully reviewed the technical content of the manuscript; and Elaine Foster and Valerie Brewster, whose questions and comments helped me see the manuscript from the reader's point of view.

Thanks are also due to Bret Rohmer and his fine production staff. Jeanne Tennant produced the layout and the technical drawings; Judy Wohlfrom was responsible for the pasteup; Mati Sikk performed his usual miracles at the phototypesetting equipment; and Hilda van Genderen and Cheryl Wilcox painstakingly proofread the book through each stage of production. The imaginative cover art is by Daniel Le Noury.

Introduction

COMPUTER LITERACY is fast becoming an essential qualification for anyone working in the business world. As more and more business tasks are aided or directed by computers—from word processing to decision making—business professionals at every level are learning more about the powers and limitations of this "new machine" in our midst.

One way to find out what a computer can do is to learn to program. This book is a business-oriented introduction to computer programming in BASIC, which continues to be the most popular language available for microcomputers. In this simple, yet surprisingly powerful language, beginning programmers can quickly learn to write significant application programs.

The goal of this book, then, is to train business professionals to read, write, and "debug" BASIC programs for business applications; that is, to help them become literate in business computing. Each chapter focuses on one syntactical feature of BASIC and presents at least one significant program to illustrate how that feature is used.

The program examples are all presented for their instructional value. This book is not a collection of ready-made, "black box" programs offered without explanation, but rather a guide to writing usable programs. Many programs are accompanied by brief descriptions of the business tasks they are designed to perform. These familiar accounting tasks are summarized to help explain what the programs do, and to demonstrate the importance of *defining* a problem before writing a program to solve it.

Chapter 1—*A First Look at BASIC*—provides an introductory overview of the programming concepts and vocabulary covered in this book. A first program is presented (the cost-of-goods-sold program), though emphasis at this point is on understanding the general organization rather than the specific details of the program.

Chapter 2—*Beginning Concepts*—introduces input and output in BASIC. Special features such as **TAB** and **PRINT USING** are discussed in detail; these features aid the programmer in producing attractive and readable reports. (We also discuss how to get along without these features in a version of BASIC that does not have them.) Additional topics of this chapter are variables, assignment statements, operations, decisions, and transfer of control. All this new material is brought together in the comparative income statement program, presented and discussed in detail in this chapter.

Chapter 3—**FOR** *Loops*—describes iteration in BASIC; that is, how to instruct the computer to perform the same command many times. A monthly sales report program is presented in two forms, first to produce a simple report, and then to produce a bar graph of monthly sales.

Chapter 4—*Arrays*—explains how to organize groups of related data conveniently in BASIC. An array is a *data structure* that requires precise syntax and a certain conceptual background, which is provided in this chapter. The power of arrays is illustrated in the present value program.

Chapter 5—*Subroutines and Program Structure*—moves step by step through a simplified general ledger program to teach the important concepts of *top-down, modular* programming. This chapter shows how to write programs that are readable and easily debugged.

Chapter 6—*Arithmetic Functions*—begins with a description of built-in functions and how they might be used in business applications. Following this is an introduction to user-defined functions, which allow the programmer to create arithmetic functions that are not included in the language itself. Among the several programs in this chapter is one that produces a break-even point graph for cost-volume-profit analysis.

Chapter 7—*Strings*—presents a number of functions that operate on, or return information about, strings of characters in BASIC. Two programs are developed for exploring the ASCII code. *Sorting* (i.e., arranging information in a given order) is also introduced, and the personnel list program illustrates the concepts presented in this chapter.

The programs in this book were written and developed on TRS- 80 and Apple II computers. Many minor differences between "versions" of BASIC are noted, and you are often directed to see how your BASIC handles a particular feature. The best place to read this book is in front of your own computer, so you can try out each program as it is presented in the book.

Exercises at the end of each chapter will guide you in further exploring the characteristics of BASIC and in approaching new applications. Appendix A contains suggested answers to some of these exercises, including several new programs.

An additional feature of this book will help you place your new understanding of BASIC in the broader context of business programming. Short optional sections appear near the end of every chapter, comparing the features of BASIC with other languages that are familiar to the business world—COBOL, Pascal, and FORTRAN. The goal is to clarify some of the relative advantages of each of these languages and to point out what they have in common with each other and with BASIC. To complement these chapter-by-chapter descriptions, Appendix B presents one complete program in each of these languages. While none of this is meant to replace formal introductions to COBOL, Pascal, and FORTRAN, this material may help you decide what language to study after mastering BASIC.

The *reserved words* of all four of the languages discussed in this book have been set in **boldface** type.

All in all, this book is designed to demystify programming for the business professional, and to serve as a guide to beginning business programming in BASIC.

CHAPTER 1

A First Look at BASIC

APPROACHING A FIRST COMPUTER LANGUAGE, we are faced with learning *two* new sets of vocabulary. One set involves the programming language itself, which has not only its own vocabulary, but also its own syntax and structure. The second set of vocabulary comprises all the terms that computer programmers use when they talk about the details of their work. In Chapter 1 we will begin learning some of these terms, even as we take a first broad look at BASIC. Our aim will be to prepare for a more detailed investigation of BASIC programming in later chapters of this book.

First BASIC Program: Cost of Goods Sold

The program we will be studying in this chapter performs three main tasks:

- It *prompts* the user to type in the inventory and sales data that the program requires as input.

- It calculates two new values—the cost of goods sold (which we will refer to as COGS), and the gross margin on sales—from the input data.

- Finally, it displays a well-organized report of both the input data and the calculated values.

Although this program is simple, it will serve to illustrate a number of important concepts; examining it, we will begin to understand how programs are written and organized in BASIC. An accompanying *flowchart* will help us conceptualize the *control structures* of the language. An examination of the output from this program will lead us to our first discussion of one of the continuing themes of this book: the importance of planning clear, well-organized and attractive output formats when programming for business applications.

The program *listing* appears in Figure 1.1. (A listing is simply a display of the lines of a program.) The first thing to notice is that all the lines of a BASIC program are numbered. The *lines of code,* as we sometimes call them, are always numbered in ascending order, although the numbering need not be in uniform multiples. In the COGS program the numbers are all multiples of 10, but this is an arbitrary choice. They could just as well have been in multiples of 5 or 50 or 100, or in uneven (ascending) intervals. It is good programming practice, however, to leave "room" between lines for insertion of new lines of code. This is because we often find ourselves adding lines to programs for one purpose or another. If the lines of the COGS program had been numbered sequentially from 1 to 65, it would be impossible to insert lines anywhere inside the program.

Another fact that we notice right away about this program is that most of the lines begin with the words **REM, INPUT,** or **PRINT.** All three of these words are part of the BASIC vocabulary, or what might be called the *reserved words* of the language. The prevalence of

INPUT and **PRINT** lines indicates what we have already mentioned about this program—that it mainly performs input/output operations. The **REM** lines are *remarks*, or comments, about the program; this feature of BASIC merits some discussion.

```
 10   REM       COGS PROGRAM
 20   REM       D. HERGERT          8 AUGUST 1981
 30   REM
 40   REM       VARIABLE NAMES
 50   REM       I                   INCOME ON SALES
 60   REM       B                   BEGINNING INVENTORY
 70   REM       P                   PURCHASES DURING PERIOD
 80   REM       E                   ENDING INVENTORY
 90   REM       C                   COST OF GOODS SOLD
100   REM       G                   GROSS MARGIN ON SALES
110   REM       A$                  ANSWER STRING
120   REM
130   REM       INPUT SECTION
140   REM
150   INPUT "INCOME ON SALES"; I
160   INPUT "BEGINNING INVENTORY"; B
170   INPUT "PURCHASES DURING PERIOD"; P
180   INPUT "ENDING INVENTORY"; E
190   REM
200   REM       CALCULATION OF COGS AND GROSS MARGIN
210   REM
220   C = B + P - E
230   G = I - C
240   REM
250   REM       OUTPUT SECTION
260   REM
270   F$ = "$$##,#####.##"
280   PRINT : PRINT
290   PRINT TAB(30); "COGS" : PRINT : PRINT
```

Figure 1.1: The Cost of Goods Sold (COGS) Program

```
300   PRINT "INCOME ON SALES"; TAB(42);
310   PRINT USING F$; I
320   GOSUB 600
330   PRINT "BEGINNING INVENTORY"; TAB(30);
340   PRINT USING F$; B
350   PRINT "PURCHASES DURING PERIOD"; TAB(30);
360   PRINT USING F$; P
370   GOSUB 600
380   PRINT "GOODS AVAILABLE FOR SALE"; TAB(30);
390   PRINT USING F$; B + P
400   PRINT "ENDING INVENTORY"; TAB(30);
410   PRINT USING F$; E
420   GOSUB 600
430   PRINT "COST OF GOODS SOLD"; TAB(42);
440   PRINT USING F$; C
450   PRINT "GROSS MARGIN ON SALES"; TAB(42);
460   PRINT USING F$; G
470   GOSUB 630
480   INPUT "ANOTHER SET OF DATA"; A$
490   IF (A$="Y") OR (A$="YES") GOTO 150
500   STOP
600   PRINT TAB(30); "- - - - - - - - - - - - - - - - - - - - - - - - - - - -"
610   PRINT
620   RETURN
630   PRINT TAB(30); "= = = = = = = = = = = = = = = = = = = = = = = = = ="
640   PRINT
650   RETURN
```

Figure 1.1: The Cost of Goods Sold (COGS) Program (cont.)

REM: Documenting a BASIC Program

The lines that begin with **REM** are not part of the programmer's instructions to the computer. Rather, they are an aid to anyone who might someday want to understand the program (including the original programmer six or eight months after the program is written). Anything at all can be written on the **REM** lines, and there is no "standard" way of writing comments for a program. Although BASIC programs are not especially hard to read, some features of the language can cause confusion and complicate the task of figuring out what the program does. A good BASIC programmer will recognize these difficult features and *document* them—in the form of **REM** comments—for the benefit of anyone who might, in the future, need to understand how the program is organized.

In the COGS program we see several groups of **REM** lines. The first lines identify the program, the author, and the date the program was written. The date can be an important piece of information if the program is ever revised and distributed in several different versions. Anyone who has a copy of the program should be able to tell what version it is.

The next group of **REM** lines identifies the *variables* that are used in this program. We will have more to say about variables later in this chapter; for now we only need to know that variables are used to store values used in the program. Every variable has a name; however, in most versions of BASIC, variable names are restricted to two or three characters. Other computer languages allow us to write *meaningful* variable names such as these:

        NET–INC
        NET _ INCOME
        NINCOME

In BASIC, we are more likely to be restricted to a single letter:

        N

or a single letter followed by a digit:

        N1

Since this is the case, it is often extremely valuable to provide a list of the variables used in a program, and brief explanations of what they are used for. This is the purpose of the **REM** lines under the heading VARIABLE NAMES.

Finally, we see three **REM** comments that identify sections of the program—INPUT SECTION, CALCULATION OF COGS AND GROSS

MARGIN, and OUTPUT SECTION. The words *section, routine,* and *block,* which often have specific meanings in other programming languages, are used somewhat informally in descriptions of BASIC to refer to a group of lines designed to perform a particular task. The **REM** comments of the COGS program thus divide the program into three different sections, making its organization immediately evident.

In summary, **REM** lines may be used (or not used) according to the immediate needs of the programmer and the anticipated needs of those who will later be reading the program. Each programmer must judge how much documentation is appropriate and necessary. We should note that **REM** comments do take up some space in the memory of the computer. This may be a disadvantage in a particularly long program if memory space is limited. Nevertheless, **REM** comments are strongly recommended as an important part of any BASIC program.

BASIC Input/Output

BASIC is an *interactive* programming language, which means that we can type information into the computer from the keyboard *while the program is being executed.* Another way of saying this is that a program *run* involves a *dialogue* between the *user* and the computer, guided by the program instructions. A programming language that is not interactive, that requires all data to be input before the beginning of the program run, is said to run in *batch* mode. FORTRAN and COBOL, two languages that we will periodically examine in this book, were originally designed as batch-mode languages.

The word in a BASIC program that creates dialogue is **INPUT**. We will be studying the details of this instruction in Chapter 2. For now, notice that the COGS program has four **INPUT** lines: lines 150 to 180. As we will see, each of these lines produces a prompt that tells the user what data to type into the computer. For example:

BEGINNING INVENTORY?

The phrase "BEGINNING INVENTORY" lets the user know exactly what data to input at this point in the dialogue. The question mark is supplied by many versions of BASIC so that the user knows that the program is waiting for input.

The **PRINT** statement, another instruction we will be mastering in Chapter 2, produces *output* from BASIC. Depending on what kind of output device the computer is connected to, the **PRINT** statement might produce a line of text on a screen or an actual line of print on a printer.

The **PRINT** statement can appear as the only word of a line of code. It then produces a blank line in the output. Notice line 280 of the COGS program:

```
280   PRINT : PRINT
```

The colon in BASIC separates two instructions in a single line of code. (Some versions of BASIC use the backslash (\) instead of the colon.) Line 280 thus produces two blank lines in the output.

When we run our COGS program to examine a sample dialogue and the resulting output, we will see the actual results of the **PRINT** and **INPUT** statements. Before we do, however, we must master a few more programming terms.

Versions of BASIC

We have referred several times to different *versions* of BASIC. Since we are about to run our first program, this is a good opportunity to discuss the meaning of that expression. The explanation will divert us from our program for a moment.

BASIC, like FORTRAN, COBOL, and Pascal, is a *high-level* language. The instructions of these languages are in English, making programming relatively "natural" for human beings. However, the *machine code,* representing the instructions that the computer actually carries out, is not in English or any other human language, but rather in strings of 0s and 1s called *binary code.* The link between a high-level language and machine language is a program itself; this program is called either a *compiler* or an *interpreter,* depending on how it ultimately supplies the machine code instructions that the computer will perform.

A compiler translates the entire program in one pass and, as long as there are no *bugs* (mistakes) in the program, creates a set of binary instructions that can be executed directly by the computer. An interpreter, on the other hand, works on one line of the program at a time, converts it into instructions the computer can perform, and then proceeds to the next line. The interpreter continues in this manner until it reaches a line that has a syntactical error (at which point execution will be terminated) or until it completes the program.

BASIC was originally designed as an interpreted language, and most versions of BASIC on the market today are interpreters rather than compilers. When we refer to different BASICs, we are, therefore, actually talking about different commercial versions of the BASIC interpreter. As we begin to learn the reserved words and the syntax of BASIC, we will often have occasion to note that one feature or another is *implementation-dependent*. This means that the feature may or may not be offered—or may appear in a slightly different form—in different versions of BASIC.

With that much said about compilers, interpreters, machine language, and the like, we may now return to our COGS program.

Running the COGS Program

The sample dialogue and output from the COGS program are shown in Figure 1.2. Notice that the input dialogue and the output display are separated by a space. (Recall the two **PRINT** statements of line 280.) The input dialogue consists of four prompts and four items of information that were entered from the keyboard by the person who ran this program. These data values were stored by the computer under the variable names supplied by the program, and the values were thus available for use later, during execution of subsequent instructions. For example, when the program displayed the prompt:

BEGINNING INVENTORY?

the user typed in the value 7800. This value was then stored in variable B to be used later in the program.

The output displays the results of the program. Notice that all four of the input values are incorporated into the output. This is good programming practice—the user should always be given a record (or "echo") of what was input into the program as data.

The output display also has three values that were not input by the user—GOODS AVAILABLE FOR SALE, COST OF GOODS SOLD, and GROSS MARGIN ON SALES. These values were calculated by the computer, using the input data, following the *algorithmic* instructions of the program.

Take a moment to study the output display. Notice its format. There are two columns of aligned figures, all of which have dollar signs and commas in the proper positions. Lines separate different categories of the statement, making the presentation clear and pleasing to the eye. None of this formatting happens by accident or automatically; all of it is designed and planned carefully by the programmer. In Chapter 2 we will be studying the methods of producing correct formatting in business reports.

Now let us return to our program and discuss the few lines that we have not yet studied.

Algorithms, Flowcharts, and Control Structures

The series of steps used to solve a problem are referred to as the *algorithm* for the solution of the problem. The term is broadly applied

```
INCOME ON SALES? 34590
BEGINNING INVENTORY? 7800
PURCHASES DURING PERIOD? 13450
ENDING INVENTORY? 1540


                               COGS


   INCOME ON SALES                          $34,590.00
                                  -------------------------

   BEGINNING INVENTORY            $7,800.00
   PURCHASES DURING PERIOD        $13,450.00
                                  -------------------------

   GOODS AVAILABLE FOR SALE       $21,250.00
   ENDING INVENTORY               $1,540.00
                                  -------------------------

   COST OF GOODS SOLD                       $19,710.00
   GROSS MARGIN ON SALES                    $14,880.00
                                  =========================

   ANOTHER SET OF DATA? N
```

Figure 1.2: Output from COGS Program

to any step-by-step solution of a problem, but in the context of computer programming it refers to the solution of a problem by a program. A program implements, or carries out the steps of, its algorithm. The main mathematical algorithm of the COGS program solves the following problem:

> Given four items of information about sales and inventory for a given period:
>
> 1. income on sales
> 2. beginning inventory
> 3. purchases during period
> 4. ending inventory
>
> find the cost of goods sold and the gross margin on sales for this period.

The algorithm for solving this problem can be expressed as follows:

> Cost of goods sold = (beginning inventory +
> purchases during period) −
> ending inventory
>
> Gross margin on sales = income on sales − COGS

It is not very hard to find the lines in the COGS program that express this algorithm in BASIC:

```
220   C = B + P − E
230   G = I − C
```

The letters C, B, P, E, G, and I are the names given to the variables in this program. They are all *real* variables, meaning variables that store real numbers. As we will see in Chapter 2, most BASICs have two other variable *types—integer* variables and *string* variables—and the types are *declared* in the name of the variable itself. Before we are finished with our discussion of the COGS program, we will see two examples of string variables.

Actually, the mathematical algorithm of the COGS program is only a part of a larger algorithm. If we think of the entire task of the program as one of printing out a statement of financial information about sales, then the complete algorithm of the task can be expressed in the following steps:

1. Input financial information about sales and inventory.
2. Calculate the COGS.
3. Calculate the gross margin on sales.
4. Print out the report.

The program has two more steps that we have not discussed yet. Look back at the output (Figure 1.2) and notice the very last line:

ANOTHER SET OF DATA? N

After presenting one report, the COGS program gives the user a chance to start all over again with another set of data. (In the program run of Figure 1.2, the user typed "N" at this point, indicating that a second report was not wanted.) We must therefore add two more steps to complete the algorithm of our program:

5. Ask if another report is required.
6. If yes, go back to Step 1 and start again; if no, end the program.

Often programmers use a tool called a *flowchart* to picture the steps of an algorithm. There are many varieties of flowcharts, and many ways of using them. We will not worry about formal flowcharting methods in this book, but we will occasionally make use of a flowchart to clarify an algorithm.[1] A flowchart for the COGS program is presented in Figure 1.3.

In this flowchart, the beginning and ending points of the algorithm are represented by ovals; input/output operations, by parallelograms; decisions, by diamonds; and other instructions, by rectangles. With this simple set of graphic representations, the flowchart makes it easy to see at a glance how the program is structured.

This brings us to the subject of *control structures* in BASIC. Control structures determine the order in which the lines of a program are to be executed. In BASIC there are five control structures: *sequence, decision, iteration, jump,* and *procedure.* We will describe the general meaning of each of these terms here; in the chapters ahead we will fill in the details of how these structures are actually implemented and used in BASIC.

---

[1] For a thorough summary of flowcharting methods and standards, see N. Chapin, "Flowchart," in *Encyclopedia of Computer Science*, ed. Anthony Ralston (New York: Van Nostrand Reinhold, 1976).

The *sequence* is the simplest form of control of a program. It means that two or more lines are executed in order, the order in which they appear in the program. Most of the COGS program illustrates sequence: the order of the line numbers determines the order in which the lines are taken up.

In a *decision* the course of action is determined by the evaluation of an expression that is either *true* or *false*. Decisions are expressed in BASIC by **IF** statements. An example appears in the COGS program:

```
480   INPUT "ANOTHER SET OF DATA"; A$
490   IF (A$="Y") OR (A$="YES") GOTO 50
```

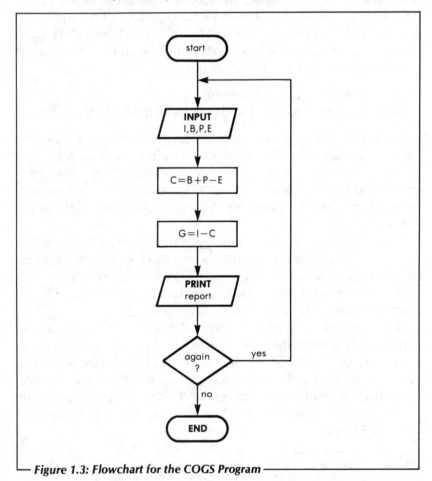

Figure 1.3: Flowchart for the COGS Program

After one report is displayed, the user is asked if there is another set of data to analyze. The user responds with a YES or a NO, and the answer is stored in the *string variable,* A$. In line 490 A$ is examined in the following expression:

(A$="Y") **OR** (A$="YES")

This expression is either true or false; that is, A$ is either storing an affirmative answer ("Y" or "YES") or it is not. What the program does next depends on the results of the evaluation of this expression. Take another look at the flowchart (Figure 1.3) to review the graphical representation of a decision. Two lines lead out of the decision diamond, one corresponding to "yes" and the other to "no."

Iteration means that one or more lines are repeated a number of times. Iterative structures are often called *loops.* In BASIC, there are two ways to implement a loop, depending on whether the number of iterations is known in advance or not. **FOR/NEXT** loops, described in Chapter 3, specify a known number of iterations. The only other way most BASICs have of expressing a loop is with a **GOTO** statement, as in line 490 of the COGS program. As long as the user types "YES" or "Y" in response to the question:

ANOTHER SET OF DATA?

then the program loops back to the input lines and begins again.

A *jump,* expressed as a **GOTO** statement, is a way of executing statements out of sequence. The **GOTO** of the COGS program is, of course, a special jump that creates a loop; however, not all **GOTO**s are used for iteration. For example, we may want to jump *forward* in a program if a certain condition is met. As we will see in Chapter 2, a **GOTO** statement combined with an **IF** is called a conditional branch or a conditional transfer of control.

Finally, *procedures,* or *subroutines,* can be used in BASIC when a set of instructions is needed in several different places in the program. We can place those lines together in a specified place in the program and use the **GOSUB** statement to *call* the subroutine; that is, to execute the lines of the subroutine whenever we need them. Control returns to the line after the **GOSUB** when the subroutine is finished. The COGS program has two subroutines that are called from the output routine. The subroutines begin at lines 600 and 630, and perform the simple task of printing lines to separate different parts of the output report. In a flowchart, we will use a special "framed" rectangle to represent a subroutine, as illustrated in Figure 1.4.

Thus, each of BASIC's five control structures—sequence, decision, iteration, jump, and procedure (or subroutine)—is implemented with specific BASIC reserved words and syntax. These five ways of controlling the action of a program—and carrying out an algorithm— may seem a bit confusing at the moment, after this quick outline. But the structures will become clearer as we study them in detail and see examples of their use in the chapters to come.

Formatting

Before we leave the COGS program, we should notice one last detail. Line 270 stores a value in the string variable F$:

    270   F$ = "$$##,#####.##"

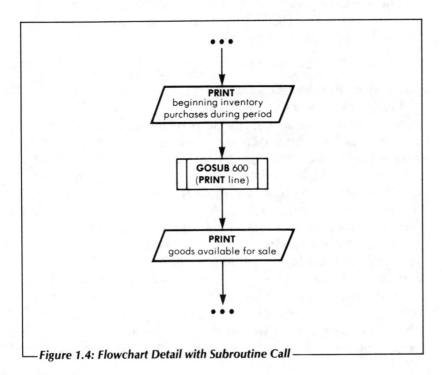

Figure 1.4: Flowchart Detail with Subroutine Call

This string of special characters is a *formatting* string. By referring to it in a **PRINT USING** instruction, we can transform a real number such as:

17203.11

into a monetary figure:

$17,203.11

This is an important feature for business programs, and is another topic we will cover in Chapter 2. We should note here, however, that not all BASICs have this feature.

Other Languages: COBOL, Pascal, and FORTRAN

We will conclude each chapter of this book with a short section describing some of the features of three additional high-level computer languages. In every case, these sections may be skipped without any loss of understanding of the BASIC material. However, by comparing BASIC with other important languages we can enhance our understanding of the advantages—and in some cases, the limitations—of BASIC programming. Also, it is often a natural step to move on to other computer languages after mastering a first one. Thus, these sections offer a very brief and informal introduction to three languages that are likely to be of interest to the business programmer.

COBOL (COmmon Business Oriented Language) is the language most widely used on large computers for business applications. A COBOL program is divided into four *divisions*—**IDENTIFICATION**, **ENVIRONMENT**, **DATA**, and **PROCEDURE**. Variables are declared and defined in the **DATA** division, and algorithmic instructions are written in the **PROCEDURE** division. COBOL is characterized by statements that are often very close to ordinary English. For example:

MULTIPLY HOURS–WORKED **BY** PAYRATE **GIVING** GROSS–SALARY.

Pascal is the most recently developed of these languages, and was originally designed as a teaching language, to teach computer programming in a systematic, structured manner. Pascal's popularity among programmers and computer hobbyists may be explained in part by its recent appearance in microcomputer versions.

FORTRAN (FORmula TRANslation), the oldest of the languages we will be discussing, is most often associated with scientific applications. However, many business applications that involve quantitative analysis—such as simulation and decision models, and problems involving statistical analysis—are written in FORTRAN.

Superficially, FORTRAN is often the language that looks most like BASIC, but we will be discussing some important differences between the two languages.

We will be seeing examples of instruction statements from all three of these languages. A complete program example written in each language can be found in Appendix B.

Summary

BASIC is an interactive high-level computer language; most versions of BASIC are interpreted rather than compiled. The control structures that determine the algorithm of a BASIC program are sequence, decision, iteration, jump, and procedure. Each of these structures can be represented graphically on a flowchart, a tool often used to clarify the action of a program.

As we saw illustrated in the output of the COGS program, BASIC provides some powerful features for formatting lines of output. These features are particularly important in creating business reports.

The COGS program, simple as it is, has served its purpose as an introduction to programming concepts. Now that we have seen it as a complete program on its own, we will be revising it slightly and incorporating it into a much larger and more significant program in Chapter 2.

Exercises

* 1.1: *Give a brief definition for each of the following terms:*

> *listing*
> *reserved word*
> *interactive*
> *high-level language*
> *machine language*
> *interpreter*
> *compiler*
> *bug*

1.2: *Draw a flowchart for some everyday event or activity (making a telephone call, starting a car, beginning a work day, etc.) Try to include all of the flowchart elements described in this chapter.*

1.3: *In this chapter we have begun to build a passive BASIC vocabulary (i.e., words we recognize, but cannot necessarily use actively). Describe the use of the following BASIC reserved words:*

REM

PRINT

INPUT

GOSUB

RETURN

GOTO

IF

*1.4: *What is the purpose of lines 480 to 500 of the COGS program?*

1.5: *What is a control structure? What are the five control structures used in BASIC?*

1.6: *Why is program documentation important? What form does documentation take in the program itself?*

---

*Answer appears in Appendix A.

CHAPTER 2

Beginning Concepts

IN CHAPTER 1 WE OUTLINED the five algorithmic control structures of a BASIC computer program. Now we will begin to fill in the details of how these patterns are implemented.

The main program of this chapter produces a comparative income statement for two consecutive years. In the course of developing this program, we will explore a wide range of BASIC features. We will start with the essentials: assignment statements, variable types, and arithmetic operations in BASIC. Then we will examine the BASIC syntax for input and output operations. We will continue to discuss an issue that must always preoccupy a good programmer: producing well-organized, readable and attractive output. Some powerful BASIC features are available to aid the programmer in this task.

Finally, we will see some examples of **IF/THEN** decisions in BASIC and the logical operations **AND, OR,** and **NOT**. We will combine **IF/THEN** statements with **GOTO** to implement conditional branching; these features will appear in the context of a routine designed to calculate the total depreciation expense of a series of depreciable items.

In addition to this depreciation routine, our income statement program makes use of a revised version of the COGS program that we examined in Chapter 1. Since over half of the program is taken up by an output routine that actually produces the income statement from the input data, we will be looking at this output routine in detail to discover the most effective ways to produce readable output.

Assignment Statements

An *assignment statement* is used to assign a value to the variable on the left of the equal sign. For example, the statement:

$$X = 2$$

assigns the value 2 to X. Notice that only a single variable name (X) appears to the left of the equal sign. The statement:

$$X + 1 = Y$$

is illegal in BASIC. The expression to the right of the equal sign, however, can be as simple or elaborate as necessary:

$$X = Y$$
$$A = (2*Y+5)^2$$
$$Q1 = X + 2$$

Most BASICs permit—and some require—the word **LET** to introduce an assignment statement:

$$\textbf{LET } D5 = A * B/2$$

The use of **LET** does not change the meaning of the statement in any way, but it may improve readability, since all other statements in BASIC begin with a reserved word.

In this chapter we will also see a form of the assignment statement that is often perplexing to beginning programmers:

$$X = X + 1$$

This statement *increments* the value of X by 1. It is equivalent to the mathematical statement:

$$x_2 = x_1 + 1$$

That is, 1 is added to the original value of x (x_1) to give a new value for x (x_2). However, in the BASIC statement, the original value of X is lost. A variable can have only one value, and a new value has been assigned to X.

If we want to save the original value of X before it is assigned a new value, we must first assign the value of X to another variable. For example:

$$U = X$$
$$X = (X + 1) * (X + 2)$$

Now, no matter what value is assigned to X, we will have a record of the original value of X in the variable U.

One final point about incrementing variables: we will often talk about *initializing* a variable to zero before an incrementation process:

$$X = 0$$

Even though most BASICs automatically initialize new variables to zero each time a program is run, initialization is a good programming habit to develop.

Variable Types

As we discussed in Chapter 1, the three variable types in BASIC are strings, integers, and reals. The type of a variable is *declared* in the name of the variable itself.

A dollar-sign suffix indicates a string variable:

$$G\$ = \text{``GROSS SALES''}$$

A string is a sequence of characters; the allowable length of a string is implementation-dependent.

For BASICs that have the integer type, a percent sign is used to declare an integer variable:

$$Y1\% = 1981$$

Integers in most BASICs must fall between -32768 and $+32767$.

A variable with neither a % nor a $ suffix in its name is a real (or *floating point*) variable:

$$D1 = 1925.23$$

The range of real numbers in BASIC is implementation-dependent and is discussed in Exercise 2.3.

Arithmetic Operations

The arithmetic operations are represented in BASIC by the following symbols:

+   addition
−   subtraction (or negation)
∗   multiplication
/   division
^   exponentiation

The order in which these operations are performed is:

1. exponentiation
2. multiplication and division, from left to right
3. addition and subtraction, from left to right.

Thus, the statement:

$$X = A + B * C/D * E^2$$

would be performed as:

$$X = A + \left(\frac{BC}{D}\right) E^2 \tag{1}$$

Parentheses take the highest precedence. That is, they are used to change the established order of these operations. For example:

$$X = (((A + B) * C) / (D * E))^2$$

means:

$$X = \left(\frac{(A + B)C}{DE}\right)^2 \tag{2}$$

Obviously, Equations 1 and 2 are quite different; this illustrates the importance of determining and expressing the correct order of operations for any problem.

Parentheses can also be added to a statement simply to improve readability. For example:

$$D1 = (V1 * (C/U)) + D1$$

In this statement, the parentheses do not change the mathematical meaning of the expression to the right of the equal sign, but they may clarify the function of the statement.

The INPUT Statement

The simplest form of the **INPUT** statement is:

INPUT A

where A is a variable name of any type. The result of this statement in most BASICs is to produce a question mark on the screen (or other output device). This prompt simply indicates that the BASIC program is waiting for the user to type in a value for the variable A:

? 3.14

In this case, the value 3.14 is assigned to the variable A.

One **INPUT** statement may contain several variables, separated by commas:

INPUT A, B$, C%

This line expects three values to be input—a real number, a string, and an integer, in that order:

? 1.49, 12-INCH RULERS, 100

Notice that the three values input for the variables A, B$, and C% are themselves separated by commas. In this case, the real number 1.49 is assigned to A, the string "12-INCH RULERS" is assigned to B$, and the integer 100 is assigned to C%.

If the value that is input does not correspond in type to the variable that is to be assigned a value, different BASICs react differently. Some BASICs conveniently print an error message, and give the user another chance, without interrupting the program. For example, let us assume we have the line:

INPUT A

in a program. In response to the prompt we type the string:

? 12-INCH RULERS

Since A is a real variable, it cannot hold a string value. The reaction of some BASICs might be something like:

        ?REDO

        ?

or:

        ✱✱✱ SYNTAX ERR

        RETYPE LINE

        ?

In both of these cases, the question mark prompt reappears, and BASIC waits for the user to try again.

   If the input line contains a string variable name, then nearly any value can be typed in to be stored in that variable. However, if a number is stored as a string, it must be treated in the program as a string, not as a number. A few string characters require special treatment. For example, if a comma appears in an input string, the whole input string must be typed between quotes:

        ? "DAVEY'S, INC."

Otherwise, the comma will appear to be separating two different input values.

   Many BASICs allow the **INPUT** line to include a prompt string, which will then be displayed before the program waits for the input values:

        INPUT "UNIT PRICE, DESCRIPTION, UNITS IN STOCK";A,B$,C%

This line produces the prompt:

        UNIT PRICE, DESCRIPTION, UNITS IN STOCK?

and waits for the user to input three values: a real number, a string, and an integer. Notice that the prompt string is in quotes in the **INPUT** statement. The closing quotation mark is followed by a semicolon. (Note two implementation variations: (1) some BASICs require a comma rather than a semicolon after the closing quotation mark; (2) some BASICs do not display a question mark at the end of the prompt.)

   We will be seeing the **INPUT** statement with a prompt string several times in the main program of this chapter. For example:

        500   **INPUT** "DO YOU HAVE DEPRECIATION EXPENSES"; A$

and

        520   **INPUT** "PERCENT INCOME TAX"; T%

The PRINT Statement

The **PRINT** statement produces output from a BASIC program. This statement includes a wide variety of different features depending on the version of BASIC being used. Some of the features described in this section are not available in all BASICs; but since output formatting features are essential in business programs, the availability of these features is an important criterion in deciding which BASIC to use.

The **PRINT** statement in its simplest form is:

> **PRINT** A

where A is a variable, a literal string (in quotes), a number, or an arithmetic expression. Examples:

```
10   PRINT X%
20   PRINT "OPERATING EXPENSES"
30   PRINT 15.23
40   PRINT (1 + I/100)^N
```

Line 10 displays the current value of X%; line 20 prints the words:

> OPERATING EXPENSES

Line 30 prints the number 15.23. Line 40 first evaluates the arithmetic expression and then prints the result. Each of these statements displays its output on a new line; that is, a *line feed* (or carriage return) is executed at the end of each line. To suppress the line feed, we simply end the **PRINT** statement with a semicolon:

```
10   PRINT "HOW MANY VALUES";
20   INPUT V%
```

These two statements produce the prompt:

> HOW MANY VALUES?

and wait for an input value for V%. Without the semicolon in line 10, however, the prompt display would be:

> HOW MANY VALUES
> ?

Multiple output values on a **PRINT** line may be separated by either a semicolon or a comma, but the results differ depending on both the punctuation chosen and the type of variable being displayed. The situation is further complicated by the fact that different versions of BASIC tend to space output differently; one of the best ways to find out exactly what any given BASIC does is through experimentation (see Exercise 2.1). In general, however, a semicolon between output values displays those values without spaces in between; a comma places values at *pre-set tab stops*.

Examine the following **PRINT** lines and the output that they produce in one version of BASIC:

```
10    PRINT "A"; "B"; "C"; "D"
20    PRINT 1; 2; 3; 4
30    PRINT "E", "F", "G", "H"
40    PRINT 5, 6, 7, 8
50    PRINT "I",,,"J", "K"
```

ABCD			
1 2 3 4			
E	F	G	H
5	6	7	8
I			J
K			

The semicolons do indeed display the string values in unspaced sequence, as we can see in the output from line 10. Numeric values (output from line 20), however, may appear with spaces, depending on the BASIC. The output from lines 30, 40, and 50 illustrates a BASIC that has three tab stops across the screen. Notice that tab stops can be skipped simply by placing more than one comma between output values (line 50).

For situations where the pre-set tab stops are inappropriate for a desired output display, many BASICs have a **TAB** function that allows the programmer to set new tabs:

PRINT TAB(A); V

In this statement, A can be a numeric value, a variable, or an arithmetic expression (real numbers are truncated):

```
10   PRINT TAB(20); "COMPARATIVE INCOME STATEMENT"
20   PRINT TAB(X%); N$
30   PRINT TAB(X^2); "*"
```

The **TAB** function is a powerful feature; without it, line 10 would have to be written by putting 20 spaces inside the string:

```
10   PRINT"              COMPARATIVE INCOME STATEMENT"
```

Lines 20 and 30 would be more difficult. (See Exercise 3.1.)

Another extremely valuable output statement is **PRINT USING**. As we saw in Chapter 1, this statement uses a format string made up of special characters that determine how the numeric output will be displayed. The general form of this statement is:

PRINT USING F$; A

where F$ is the format string. The table in Figure 2.1 describes the most important format characters used in this statement.

The following statement illustrates the use of these characters:

PRINT USING "PAY EXACTLY **$###,###.##"; 5432.109

The output from this instruction is:

PAY EXACTLY ****$5,432.11

#	Represents one digit of the number
.	Indicates placement of decimal point
,	Causes commas to be printed every three digits to the left of the decimal; may be placed in any position in the format string
$	Puts dollar sign in position indicated
$$	Places "floating" dollar sign
**	Fills space up to the first digit with asterisks
**$	Prints asterisks before floating dollar sign

Figure 2.1: Format Characters for PRINT USING —

The decimal is rounded to the number of places indicated in the format string, in this case two.

We will see many examples of the **PRINT USING** statement in our comparative income statement program. Since we will be creating a table with three columns of figures, we will establish the format strings early in the output routine. One format string, F1$, will be used for the top and bottom lines, where a dollar sign must be printed. The other string, F2$, will be used for all the other lines:

```
F1$ = "$##,######    $##,######    $##,######"
F2$ = " ##,######    ##,######    ##,######"
```

With these strings defined, the **PRINT USING** statements are easily written; for example:

```
PRINT USING F1$; G1, G2, (G2 — G1);
```

Decisions, Logic, and Transfer of Control

Our comparative income statement program is divided into two main parts—an input routine and an output routine. The input routine prompts the user to supply information for two years' income statements, including all the data that were needed in the COGS program, plus data on operating expenses and income tax rate. The output routine arranges all the data in a readable format and calculates the "bottom lines" and the difference (increase or decrease) between the two years' data.

In this section we will examine one part of the input section, the depreciation input routine (Figure 2.4). This routine allows the user to incorporate depreciation expenses—for any number of depreciable items—into the total operating expenses for each year. (In its present form, this program simply calculates depreciation on a straight-line basis; in Chapter 4 we will examine a program that uses other depreciation methods.)

These are the steps followed by the depreciation input routine:

1. Initialize the total depreciation expense for each year (D1 and D2) to 0 (as we have noted, this is not always strictly necessary,

but it is always good programming practice); initialize the item counter (X%) to 1 (lines 1090 to 1110).

2. Prompt the user to input the original cost of an item to be depreciated; store the input value in the variable C (lines 1120 and 1130).

3. Increment the item counter (line 1140).

4. Prompt the user to input the number of years of useful life for this item; store the input value in U (line 1150).

5. Prompt the user to indicate whether the depreciation expense of this item applies to both years or only to one of the years; if only one year, prompt the user to indicate which year, and store the year in W%. Set the values of V1 and V2 (which act as "switches") accordingly (lines 1160 to 1240).

6. Calculate the depreciation expense (C/U) and add it to the total accumulated depreciation expense (D1, D2) for both years or for only one of the years, depending on the user's instructions (lines 1280 and 1290).

7. Ask the user if there is another item to depreciate; if yes, go to step 2 above, otherwise, go back to the main input routine (lines 1300 to 1330).

The flowchart for this routine is shown in Figure 2.2. We will use this routine to illustrate the BASIC decision statement, **IF/THEN**; the logical operators, **AND**, **OR** and **NOT**; and the transfer of control statement, **GOTO**.

The general form of the decision statement in BASIC is:

IF (statement1) **THEN** statement2

where statement1 (parentheses optional) is an equality, inequality, or variable that evaluates to "true" or "false," and statement2 is typically an assignment statement, an input/output statement, a transfer of control statement, or the word **STOP**, which ends the program.

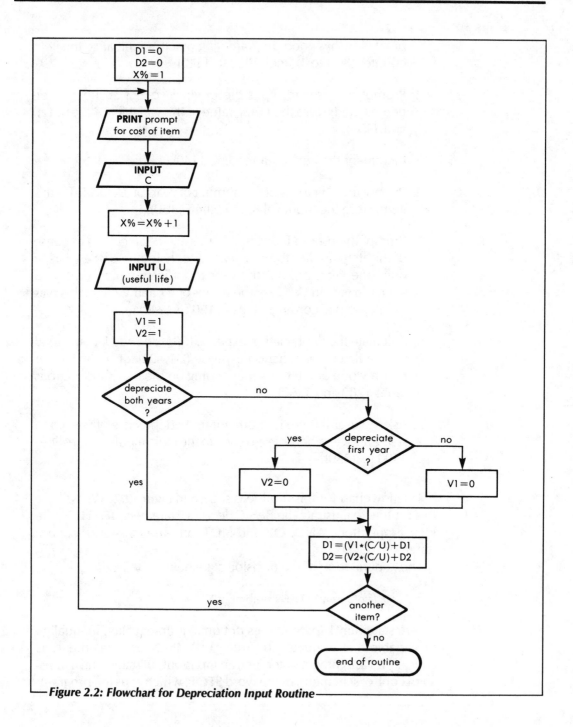

Figure 2.2: Flowchart for Depreciation Input Routine

By an equality or inequality in BASIC, we mean a statement that uses one of the following symbols:

=	equal to
<>	not equal to
<	less than
>	greater than
<=	less than or equal to
>=	greater than or equal to

Thus, given the statement:

IF (X > 100) **THEN PRINT** "X IS TOO LARGE"

BASIC assigns a "true" or a "false" to the statement (X > 100). If the statement is true, then BASIC performs the command that appears after the word **THEN**, in this case a **PRINT** statement. If, on the other hand, (X > 100) is false, then BASIC ignores the statement after **THEN** and passes on to the next line of the program.

Let us look at another example:

```
10   INPUT F$, C
20   IF (F$ = "PART#1") THEN P1 = P1 + C
```

In line 20, the statement after **IF** is an equality, and the statement after **THEN** is an assignment statement. (Note the two distinct uses in BASIC for the equal sign.) If the user inputs the word PART#1 for F$ (line 10), then the value of the variable P1 is increased by the value of C (line 20). Otherwise, the assignment statement is ignored, and BASIC goes on to the next line in the program.

We might note here that BASIC actually evaluates the statement after the **IF** as a 0 if the statement is false and a −1 or 1 (depending on the version of BASIC) if the statement is true. This is why the statement after the word **IF** can be a *variable*. (We will explore this further in Exercise 2.2, and in Chapter 5.)

The statement after **IF** can also be a multiple or complex statement, qualified by the words **AND, OR** or **NOT**. These three words are the logical "operators" in BASIC. The word **NOT** before a logical statement reverses the value of the statement. That is, it changes a "true" to a "false" or a "false" to a "true." For example:

IF NOT (D = 0) **THEN** X = N/D

If D does not equal 0, this statement performs the division, N/D, and assigns the value to X. If D *does* equal 0, then the statement **NOT** (D = 0) is false, in which case the statement after **THEN** is ignored.

AND is the logical intersection of two statements; **OR** is the logical union. This can be illustrated in any number of ways. Examine the following statements:

```
10   IF (X > = 0) AND (X < = 100) THEN PRINT "FROM 0 TO 100"
20   IF (X < 0) OR (X > 100) THEN PRINT "NEGATIVE OR OVER 100"
```

In line 10, the **PRINT** statement will be executed only if *both* (X > = 0) *and* (X < = 100) are true; in other words, if X is between 0 and 100, inclusive. In line 20, the **PRINT** statement will be executed if *either* (X < 0) *or* (X > 100) is true; that is, if X is either negative or greater than 100. The "truth tables" shown in Figure 2.3 summarize the results of logical statements that contain **AND** or **OR**.

The last BASIC statement that we must examine before looking at

AND		
1st Statement	2nd Statement	Result
true	true	true
true	false	false
false	true	false
false	false	false
OR		
1st Statement	2nd Statement	Result
true	true	true
true	false	true
false	true	true
false	false	false

Figure 2.3: Truth Tables

the depreciation input routine is the **GOTO** statement. This statement *transfers control* of the program to another line, out of sequence from the top-down flow of a BASIC program. The form of the **GOTO** statement is:

    GOTO line number

The line number can be either greater than (below) or less than (above) the line number of the **GOTO** statement itself. For example:

    200   **GOTO** 10

and

    1260   **GOTO** 1290

Upon meeting a **GOTO** statement, BASIC executes the line designated by the line number and then proceeds sequentially from there.

The obvious way to increase the power of a **GOTO** statement is to combine it with an **IF/THEN** decision. Syntactically, such a combination can take three different forms. All three of the following statements mean exactly the same thing:

    IF (W% = Y2%) **THEN GOTO** 1270
    IF (W% = Y2%) **THEN** 1270
    IF (W% = Y2%) **GOTO** 1270

In all three of these statements, if the equality turns out to be true, then control of the program is passed to line 1270.

It should be noted that the **GOTO** statement does not meet with universal approval in the programming world. Indeed, it can lead to programs that are confusing and difficult to read and to debug. Some "structured" languages—such as Pascal and COBOL—supply syntax that allows the programmer to avoid **GOTO**s in most cases. (Structured programming means much more than just avoiding **GOTO**s, however; we will discuss this topic in Chapter 5.) Unfortunately, in BASIC—or at least in most versions of BASIC—the only way to implement some algorithms is by using **GOTO**s. This does *not* mean, however, that BASIC is doomed to unintelligibility because of its **GOTO**s. The careful programmer can improve the situation by using **GOTO**s thoughtfully and supplying **REM** comments where a **GOTO** is likely to confuse someone who is reading the program. With this said, we can move on to an examination of what the **GOTO** statement can do.

The depreciation input routine is shown in Figure 2.4. (Note that this routine does not run by itself in its present form; its action is dependent on the larger comparative income statement program, of which it is a part.) Recall from the flowchart of this routine (Figure 2.2) that most of the routine is contained within a large loop, which repeats as long as the user has more depreciable items to enter into the total depreciation expense. This loop is created by the following lines:

```
1300   INPUT "ANOTHER ITEM"; A$
1310   IF (A$ = "Y") OR (A$ = "YES") GOTO 1120
```

Line 1300 produces the prompt:

ANOTHER ITEM?

Line 1310 allows either a Y or a YES to continue the routine. This choice is supplied via the **OR** operator. If there is another depreciation expense to enter, the user types Y or YES, and the **GOTO** statement transfers control of the program to line 1120, which produces a prompt for the next item:

```
1120   PRINT "ORIGINAL COST OF ITEM # "; X%;
```

Otherwise, if the user types an N or a NO (or anything else, for that matter) the program simply continues on to line 1330, which returns control to the main input routine:

```
1330   GOTO 520
```

```
1000   REM
1010   REM     DEPRECIATION INPUT ROUTINE
1020   REM     VARIABLE NAMES
1025   REM     X%            COUNTER FOR DEPRECIABLE ITEMS
1030   REM     D1, D2        DEPRECIATION EXPENSE (STRAIGHT LINE)
1040   REM     C             COST OF EQUIPMENT TO BE DEPRECIATED
1050   REM     U             USEFUL LIFE (IN YEARS)
1060   REM     V1, V2        FACTOR (0 OR 1) FOR DETERMINING TO
1070   REM                   WHICH YEAR(S) DEPRECIATION APPLIES
1080   REM
```

Figure 2.4: Depreciation Input Routine

```
1090    D1 = 0
1100    D2 = 0
1110    X% = 1
1120    PRINT "ORIGINAL COST OF ITEM # "; X%;
1130    INPUT C
1140    X% = X% + 1
1150    INPUT "YEARS USEFUL LIFE"; U
1160    V1 = 1
1170    V2 = 1
1180    INPUT "DEPRECIATE FOR BOTH YEARS"; A$
1190    IF (A$ = "Y") OR (A$ = "YES") GOTO 1280
1200    REM       ONE YEAR ONLY
1210    INPUT "DEPRECIATION FOR WHICH YEAR"; W%
1220    IF (W% <> Y1%) AND (W% <> Y2%) GOTO 1210
1230    IF (W% = Y1%) THEN V2 = 0
1240    IF (W% = Y2%) THEN V1 = 0
1250    REM
1260    REM       STRAIGHT—LINE DEPRECIATION FOR APPROPRIATE YEAR(S).
1270    REM
1280    D1 = (V1 * (C/U)) + D1
1290    D1 = (V2 * (C/U)) + D2
1300    INPUT "ANOTHER ITEM"; A$
1310    IF (A$ = "Y") OR (A$ = "YES") GOTO 1120
1320    REM       RETURN TO INPUT ROUTINE
1330    GOTO 520
```

Figure 2.4: Depreciation Input Routine (cont.)

The depreciation input routine contains two other significant uses of the **GOTO** instruction, which we will describe briefly before looking at the entire comparative income statement program.

One important type of *conditional branch* (i.e., **IF** combined with **GOTO**) is the input test. Often we need to test the appropriateness of an input value before proceeding in the program. If the value is in the range of expected values, we can continue; if not, we must loop back to the **INPUT** statement for another try. Lines 1210 and 1220 illustrate this situation:

```
1210   INPUT "DEPRECIATE FOR WHICH YEAR"; W%
1220   IF (W% <> Y1%) AND (W% <> Y2%) GOTO 1210
```

Line 1210 prompts the user to input one of the two years of the comparative income statement. As we will see when we look at the entire program, these two consecutive years (for example, 1980 and 1981) are stored in the variables Y1% and Y2%. The rest of the depreciation routine depends on the value input for W%; if a year other than Y1% or Y2% is entered, then the rest of the routine is meaningless. Therefore, line 1220 tests the value of W% to make sure that one of the two years has been input. If W% is not equal to either Y1% or Y2% (an **AND** condition), then the user has made an error; the **GOTO** statement loops back to the **INPUT** statement to prompt the user to input another value for W%.

The other important example of conditional branching in this routine is the application of the depreciation expense to the correct year (or years). The depreciation expense is calculated and added to the total depreciation expense for the year in lines 1280 and 1290:

```
1280   D1 = (V1 * (C/U)) + D1
1290   D2 = (V2 * (C/U)) + D2
```

The expression C/U represents the cost of the item divided by the number of years of useful life—the formula for straight-line depreciation (with no residual value). Notice that for both years this value is multiplied by another variable, V1 or V2. These variables are assigned the values 0 or 1, depending on whether the depreciation expense is to be added to the total or not.

V1 and V2 are initialized to 1 in lines 1160 and 1170. If the depreciation expense applies to both years, then line 1190 branches directly to the depreciation calculation:

```
1190   IF (A$ = "Y") OR (A$ = "YES") GOTO 1280
```

However, if the depreciation applies to only one year, then lines 1230 and 1240 assign the value 0 to one of the two variables, V1 or V2:

```
1230   IF (W% = Y1%) THEN V2 = 0
1240   IF (W% = Y2%) THEN V1 = 0
```

Some BASICs extend the **IF/THEN** syntax to include the word **ELSE**.

(We will see later that Pascal, COBOL, and some FORTRANs also have this feature.) In that case, lines 1230 and 1240 can be combined in a single line:

```
1230   IF (W% = Y1%) THEN V2 = 0 ELSE V1 = 0
```

The Comparative Income Statement Program

The entire listing for our program appears in Figure 2.5; a sample run is shown in Figure 2.6. The program is worth examining carefully, since it illustrates all the features we have discussed in this chapter. The following notes review the most important points:

Lines 50 to 110 set up any string values that are used more than once in the program. These particular strings are used both in the input routine and in the output routine.

The input routine (from line 290) prompts the user to input two values for each line of the income statement. For example:

```
310   PRINT G$;
320   INPUT G1, G2
```

produces the prompt:

```
GROSS SALES?
```

and waits for input values for G1 and G2. Notice that line 300 tests to make sure the years Y1 and Y2 are consecutive.

Line 450 compares the ending inventory of the first year with the beginning inventory of the second year. If they are not the same, then lines 560 to 600 allow the user to input new values if the discrepancy was unintentional.

In the output routine, lines 2130 to 2180 print the heading for the income statement. Note the use of the **TAB** function to place the column headings properly.

Each output line of the income statement is produced by four lines of code. For example:

```
2210   PRINT G$; TAB(23);
2220   PRINT USING F1$; G1, G2, ABS(G2 − G1);
2230   IF ((G2 − G1) < 0) THEN PRINT " *";
2240   PRINT
```

Line 2210 prints the category of the line (in this case "GROSS SALES") and tabs to *column* 23 (that is, the 23rd position in the output line). The semicolon at the end of line 2210 prevents a line feed. Line 2220 uses the format string, F1$, to position the three output values in the correct columns: the gross sales for each of the two years, and the difference between them. The BASIC function **ABS** produces the *absolute value* (i.e., the positive value) of the difference between the two years' gross sales. (We will study this and other BASIC functions in detail in Chapters 6 and 7.) Line 2230 flags the line with an asterisk if the value for the second year is smaller than the value for the first year. Finally, line 2240 simply produces a line feed, since both of the preceding lines of code ended in semicolons.

Lines 2360 through 2610 are similar to the COGS program of Chapter 1, except that here we are comparing the sales of two years.

Line 2530 (which can be "commented out" with the word **REM**) stops the output until the user presses the return key. This is a useful trick to aid screen-viewing of the output; the user should always be allowed to examine a full screen of information at leisure before requesting additional output.

The rest of the output routine deals with expenses and produces the subtotals and totals of the income statement.

```
 10   REM       COMPARATIVE INCOME STATEMENT PROGRAM
 20   REM       D. HERGERT        11 JULY 1981
 30   REM
 40   REM
 50   G$ = "GROSS SALES"
 60   R$ = "RETURNED SALES"
 70   B$ = "BEGINNING INVENTORY"
 80   P$ = "PURCHASES DURING PERIOD"
 90   E$ = "ENDING INVENTORY"
100   S$ = "SELLING EXPENSES"
110   M$ = "ADMIN EXPENSES"
120   INPUT "NAME OF COMPANY"; N$
130   PRINT "GIVE FINANCIAL INFORMATION FOR TWO"
140   PRINT "CONSECUTIVE YEARS."
```

Figure 2.5: Comparative Income Statement Program

```
150   REM
160   REM       INPUT ROUTINE
170   REM       VARIABLE NAMES
180   REM       Y1%, Y2%              YEARS
190   REM       G1, G2               GROSS SALES
200   REM       R1, R2               RETURNED SALES
210   REM       B1, B2               BEGINNING INVENTORY (IN $)
220   REM       P1, P2               PURCHASES DURING PERIOD (IN $)
230   REM       E1, E2               ENDING INVENTORY
240   REM       S1, S2               SELLING EXPENSES
250   REM       M1, M2               ADMINISTRATIVE EXPENSES
260   REM       T                    TAX RATE (PERCENT)
270   REM       A$                   ANSWER STRING (Y OR N)
280   REM
290   INPUT "INCOME YEARS (YYYY, YYYY)"; Y1%, Y2%
300   IF (Y1% <> Y2% − 1) GOTO 130
310   PRINT G$;
320   INPUT G1, G2
330   PRINT R$;
340   INPUT R1, R2
350   PRINT B$;
360   INPUT B1, B2
370   PRINT P$;
380   INPUT P1, P2
390   PRINT E$;
400   INPUT E1, E2
410   REM       FIND OUT IF BEGINNING INVENTORY OF SECOND
420   REM       YEAR IS SAME AS ENDING INVENTORY OF FIRST
430   REM       YEAR; IF NOT, ALERT USER TO THE
440   REM       DISCREPANCY.
450   IF B2 <> E1 THEN GOTO 550
460   PRINT S$;
470   INPUT S1, S2
480   PRINT M$;
```

Figure 2.5: Comparative Income Statement Program (cont.)

```
490    INPUT M1, M2
500    INPUT "DO YOU HAVE DEPRECIATION EXPENSES"; A$
510    IF (A$ = "Y") OR (A$ = "YES") GOTO 1010
520    INPUT "PERCENT INCOME TAX"; T
530    GOTO 2130 : REM COMPUTE AND DISPLAY INCOME STATEMENT
540    REM
550    REM      GIVE USER CHANCE TO REDO INVENTORY INPUT
560    PRINT "ENDING INVENTORY OF "; Y1%
570    PRINT "NOT EQUAL TO BEGINNING INVENTORY OF "; Y2%
580    INPUT "OK"; A$
590    IF (A$ <> "YES") AND (A$ <> "Y") THEN GOTO 350
600    GOTO 460

1000   REM
1010   REM      DEPRECIATION INPUT ROUTINE
1020   REM      VARIABLE NAMES
1030   REM      D1, D2           DEPRECIATION EXP. (STRAIGHT LINE)
1040   REM      C                COST OF EQUIPMENT
1050   REM      U                USEFUL LIFE (IN YEARS)
1060   REM      V1, V2           FACTOR (0 OR 1) FOR DETERMINING TO
1070   REM                       WHICH YEAR(S) DEPRECIATION APPLIES
1080   REM
1090   D1 = 0
1100   D2 = 0
1110   X% = 1
1120   PRINT "ORIGINAL COST OF ITEM # "; X%;
1130   INPUT C
1140   X% = X% + 1
1150   INPUT "YEARS USEFUL LIFE"; U
1160   V1 = 1
1170   V2 = 1
1180   INPUT "DEPRECIATE FOR BOTH YEARS (YES OR NO)"; A$
1190   IF (A$ = "Y") OR (A$ = "YES") GOTO 1280
1200   REM      ONE YEAR ONLY
```

Figure 2.5: Comparative Income Statement Program (cont.)

```
1210    INPUT "DEPRECIATE FOR WHICH YEAR"; W%
1220    IF (W% <> Y1%) AND (W% <> Y2%) GOTO 1210
1230    IF (W% = Y1%) THEN V2 = 0
1240    IF (W% = Y2%) THEN V1 = 0
1250    REM
1260    REM        STRAIGHT—LINE DEPRECIATION
1270    REM
1280    D1 = (V1 * (C/U)) + D1
1290    D2 = (V2 * (C/U)) + D2
1300    INPUT "ANOTHER ITEM (YES OR NO)"; A$
1310    IF (A$ = "Y") OR (A$ = "YES") GOTO 1120
1320    REM        RETURN TO INPUT ROUTINE
1330    GOTO 520

2000    REM
2010    REM        OUTPUT ROUTINE
2020    REM        VARIABLE NAMES
2030    REM        F1$, F2$            FORMAT STRINGS
2040    REM        N1, N2             NET SALES
2050    REM        Q1, Q2             GOODS AVAILABLE FOR SALE
2060    REM        C1, C2             COST OF GOODS SOLD
2070    REM        I1, I2             GROSS MARGIN ON SALES
2080    REM        Z1, Z2             TOTAL OPERATING EXPENSES
2090    REM        K1, K2             GROSS INCOME
2100    REM        L1, L2             INCOME TAX PAYABLE
2110    REM        U1, U2             NET INCOME
2120    REM
2130    PRINT TAB(20); N$
2140    PRINT TAB (20); "COMPARATIVE INCOME STATEMENT"
2150    PRINT TAB(20); "FOR THE YEARS "; Y1%; " AND "; Y2%
2160    PRINT
2170    PRINT TAB(50); "INCREASE OR"
2180    PRINT TAB(27); Y1%; TAB(40); Y2%; TAB(50); "DECREASE (*)";
```

Figure 2.5: Comparative Income Statement Program (cont.)

```
2190    F1% = "$##,######    $##,######    $##,######"
2200    F2% = " ##,######    ##,######    ##,######"
2210    PRINT G$; TAB(23);
2220    PRINT USING F1$; G1, G2, ABS(G2 — G1);
2230    IF ((G2 — G1) < 0) THEN PRINT " *";
2240    PRINT
2250    PRINT "  LESS RETURNS"; TAB(23);
2260    PRINT USING F2$; R1, R2, ABS(R2 — R1);
2270    IF ((R2 — R1) < 0) THEN PRINT " *";
2280    PRINT
2290    PRINT "NET SALES"; TAB(23);
2300    N1 = G1 — R1
2310    N2 = G2 — R2
2320    PRINT USING F2$; N1, N2, ABS(N2 — N1);
2330    IF ((N2 — N1) < 0) THEN PRINT " *";
2340    PRINT
2350    PRINT
2360    PRINT "COST OF GOODS SOLD"
2370    PRINT "  BEGINNG INVENTORY"; TAB(23);
2380    PRINT USING F2$; B1, B2
2390    PRINT "  PURCHASES"; TAB(23);
2400    PRINT USING F2$; P1, P2
2410    PRINT "  GOODS AVAILABLE"; TAB(23);
2420    Q1 = B1 + P1
2430    Q2 = B2 + P2
2440    PRINT USING F2$; Q1, Q2
2450    PRINT " "; E$; TAB(23);
2460    PRINT USING F2$; E1, E2
2470    C1 = Q1 — E1
2480    C2 = Q2 — E2
2490    PRINT "COST OF GOODS SOLD"; TAB(23);
2500    PRINT USING F2$; C1, C2, ABS(C2 — C1);
2510    IF ((C2 — C1) < 0) THEN PRINT " *";
```

Figure 2.5: Comparative Income Statement Program (cont.)

```
2520    PRINT
2530    INPUT "CONTINUE"; 0$
2540    PRINT
2550    I1 = N1 − C1
2560    I2 = N2 − C2
2570    PRINT "GROSS MARGIN ON SALES"; TAB(23);
2580    PRINT USING F2$; I1, I2, ABS(I2 − I1);
2590    IF ((I2 − I1) < 0) THEN PRINT " *";
2600    PRINT
2610    PRINT
2620    PRINT "OPERATING EXPENSES"
2630    PRINT " "; S$; TAB(23);
2640    PRINT USING F2$; S1, S2, ABS(S2 − S1);
2650    IF ((S2 − S1) < 0) THEN PRINT " *";
2660    PRINT
2670    PRINT " "; M$; TAB(23);
2680    PRINT USING F2$; M1, M2, ABS(M2 − M1);
2690    IF ((M2 − M1) < 0) THEN PRINT " *";
2700    PRINT
2710    PRINT " DEPRECIATION EXP"; TAB(23);
2720    PRINT USING F2$; D1, D2, ABS(D2 − D1);
2730    IF ((D2 − D1) < 0) THEN PRINT " *";
2740    PRINT
2750    Z1 = S1 + M1 + D1
2760    Z2 = S2 + M2 + D2
2770    PRINT "TOTAL OPERATING"
2780    PRINT " EXPENSES"; TAB(23);
2790    PRINT USING F2$; Z1, Z2, ABS(Z2 − Z1);
2800    IF ((Z2 − Z1) < 0) THEN PRINT " *";
2810    PRINT
2820    PRINT
2830    K1 = I1 − Z1
2840    K2 = I2 − Z2
```

Figure 2.5: Comparative Income Statement Program (cont.)

```
2850    PRINT "GROSS INCOME"; TAB(23);
2860    PRINT USING F1$; K1, K2, ABS(K2 — K1);
2870    IF ((K2 — K1)< 0) THEN PRINT " *";
2880    PRINT
2890    PRINT "INCOME TAX AT "; T; "%"; TAB(23);
2900    L1 = K1 * (T/100)
2910    L2 = K2 * (T/100)
2920    PRINT USING F2$; L1, L2, ABS(L2 — L1);
2930    IF ((L2 — L1)< 0) THEN PRINT " *";
2940    PRINT
2950    PRINT "NET  INCOME"; TAB(23);
2960    U1 = K1 — L1
2970    U2 = K2 — L2
2980    PRINT USING F1$; U1, U2, ABS(U2 — U1);
2990    IF ((U1 — U1)< 0) THEN PRINT " *";
3000    PRINT
3010    PRINT
3020    END
```

Figure 2.5: Comparative Income Statement Program (cont.)

```
NAME OF COMPANY? "SMITH'S, INC."
GIVE FINANCIAL INFORMATION FOR TWO
CONSECUTIVE YEARS.
INCOME YEARS (YYYY, YYYY)? 1980, 1981
GROSS SALES? 2478, 3219
RETURNED SALES? 11, 9
BEGINNING INVENTORY? 576, 420
PURCHASES DURING PERIOD? 1204, 1300
ENDING INVENTORY? 420, 123
SELLING EXPENSES? 24, 33
ADMIN EXPENSES? 29, 31
DO YOU HAVE DEPRECIATION EXPENSES? Y
ORIGINAL COST OF ITEM # 1 ? 110
YEARS USEFUL LIFE? 5
DEPRECIATE FOR BOTH YEARS (YES OR NO)? Y
ANOTHER ITEM (YES OR NO)? Y
ORIGINAL COST OF ITEM # 2 ? 85
YEARS USEFUL LIFE? 7
DEPRECIATE FOR BOTH YEARS (YES OR NO)? N
DEPRECIATE FOR WHICH YEAR? 1981
ANOTHER ITEM (YES OR NO)? N
PERCENT INCOME TAX? 35
```

Figure 2.6: Output from Comparative Income Statement Program

```
                      SMITH'S, INC.
                      COMPARATIVE INCOME STATEMENT
                      FOR THE YEARS   1980   AND   1981

                                                         INCREASE OR
                                 1980           1981     DECREASE (*)
   GROSS SALES          $       2,478    $     3,219    $      741
     LESS RETURNS                  11              9              2 *
   NET SALES                    2,467          3,210            743

   COST OF GOODS SOLD
     BEGINNG INVENTORY           576            420
     PURCHASES                 1,204          1,300
     GOODS AVAILABLE           1,780          1,720
     ENDING INVENTORY           420            123
   COST OF GOODS SOLD         1,360          1,597            237
   CONTINUE?

   GROSS MARGIN ON SALES      1,107          1,613            506

   OPERATING EXPENSES
     SELLING EXPENSES            24             33              9
     ADMIN EXPENSES              29             31              2
     DEPRECIATION EXP            22             34             12
   TOTAL OPERATING
     EXPENSES                    75             98             23

   GROSS INCOME          $     1,032    $     1,515    $      483
   INCOME TAX AT   35 %         361            530            169
   NET INCOME            $       671    $       985    $      314
```

Figure 2.6: Output from Comparative Income Statement Program (cont.)

Other Languages

In a COBOL program, variables are defined in the **DATA DIVISION**. The maximum number of digits or characters that a variable can hold is specified in a **PIC** statement, and the variable can be initialized in a **VALUE** statement:

WORKING STORAGE SECTION.

77 WS-AMT-OF-SALE	**PIC** 999V99.	
77 WS-RECORDS-PROCESSED	**PIC** 999	**VALUE ZEROS.**
77 WS-END-OF-FILE	**PIC** XXX	**VALUE SPACES.**

Digits are represented by 9s in the **PIC** statement and the position of the decimal is indicated by a V. Characters are represented by Xs. Output formatting features similar to BASIC are also available; for example, the floating dollar sign with commas:

    05   SALES-AMOUNT   **PIC** $$$,$$$.99.

Variables are assigned values in the **PROCEDURE DIVISION**, with a **MOVE** statement. The following statement initializes WS-AMT-OF-SALE to zero:

  MOVE ZEROS TO WS-AMT-OF-SALE.

Other statements, including **ADD** and **COMPUTE**, are used to assign computed values to a variable:

  COMPUTE WS-AMT-OF-SALE **ROUNDED** =
      QUANTITY-SOLD **OF** INVOICE-CARD *
      UNIT-PRICE **OF** INVOICE-CARD.
  ADD WS-AMT-OF-SALE **TO** WS-AMT-OF-INVOICE.
  ADD 1 **TO** WS-RECORDS-PROCESSED.

The COBOL **READ** statement reads an input record for which the significance of each column or group of columns has been defined in the **DATA DIVISION**:

  READ CARD-FILE, **AT END MOVE** 'YES' **TO** WS-END-OF-FILE.

The **WRITE** statement produces an output record:

  MOVE HEADING-LINE **TO** PRINT-LINE.
  WRITE PRINT-REC **AFTER ADVANCING** 3 **LINES**.

Finally, here is an example of the **IF/ELSE** statement in COBOL:

  IF RC-RESPONSE = 'Y'
      ADD 1 **TO** RESPONSE-ONE
  ELSE
      IF RC-RESPONSE = 'N'
          ADD 1 **TO** RESPONSE-TWO
      ELSE
          ADD 1 **TO** RESPONSE-THREE.

One additional note about COBOL: unlike BASIC, FORTRAN, or Pascal, COBOL has very exacting rules about spacing. For example, the operators (+, −, *, and /) and the equal sign must have spaces both before and after they appear. Failure to follow these rules perfectly means the program will not run.

In Pascal, all variables are defined in the **TYPE** and **VAR** sections in the "heading" of the program:

```
VAR
    WHICH, YEAR1, YEAR2,
    V1, V2 :   INTEGER;
    DEPRECIATION :   REAL;
    ANSWER :   CHAR;
```

Assignment statements are indicated by a colon and equal sign together:

```
V1 := 1;
V2 := 1;
```

This form distinguishes assignment statements from "Boolean" equalities:

```
IF (WHICH = YEAR1) THEN V2 := 0
ELSE V1: = 1;
```

The READ, READLN, WRITE, and WRITELN statements are used for input/output in Pascal:

```
REPEAT
    WRITE ('DEPRECIATE FOR BOTH YEARS? ');
    READLN (ANSWER)
UNTIL (ANSWER = 'Y') OR (ANSWER = 'N');
```

Although Pascal has a **GOTO** statement, its use is avoided whenever possible. Note the use of **REPEAT/UNTIL** in the statement above to validate the input.

In FORTRAN, variables beginning with the letters I, J, K, L, M, and N are automatically integers unless defined otherwise by the programmer. **READ** and **WRITE** statements are always associated with **FORMAT** statements that indicate how variables are to be handled in input and output. The **FORMAT** statement has a special syntax of its own that seems somewhat cryptic to the uninitiated, but takes little effort to learn. Examples:

>   **READ** (5,110) P, N, R
> 110   **FORMAT** (F7.0, I2, F3.1)
>   **WRITE** (6, 130) J
> 130   **FORMAT** ('1', 110X, 'PAGE ', I2)

The **READ** statement above reads values for three variables from a data card: P, a real variable (7 digits); I, an integer (2 digits); and R, a real (3 digits altogether, 1 digit after the decimal point). The **WRITE** statement starts at the top of a new page ('1'), skips 110 spaces (110X), writes the word PAGE, and then prints the value of the integer variable J. Notice that **FORMAT** statements are numbered, and these line numbers are referenced in the **READ** and **WRITE** statements.

FORTRAN uses different symbols than BASIC and Pascal for equalities and inequalities:

FORTRAN	BASIC
.EQ.	=
.NE.	<>
.LT.	<
.GT.	>
.LE.	<=
.GE.	>=

Examples of **IF** statements in FORTRAN:

> **IF** (OLDP .GT. P) GO TO 179
> **IF** (N .EQ. 4) G = 4.0
> **IF** (D .GT. 3) **WRITE** (6,150)

Summary

Although we have discussed a lot of material in this chapter, it will all seem second nature as soon as we have practiced it a bit. We began with a discussion of assignment statements, variable types, and arithmetic operations in BASIC. Then we saw the powerful input/output syntax that BASIC offers, including such capabilities as:

• Using an **INPUT** statement to print a prompt.

- Producing appropriate output with the **TAB** function, and with punctuation in the **PRINT** statement.

- Formatting special characters in numerical output with the important **PRINT USING** statement.

Finally, we went into the details of **IF/THEN** decisions, and the logical operators **AND**, **OR**, and **NOT**. We learned how to combine **IF/THEN** with **GOTO** to implement a *conditional branch*.

Try to become familiar with all of these features before continuing on to the next chapter. The best way to review the material of this chapter is to study the comparative income statement program, which illustrates everything we have discussed so far.

Exercises

2.1: *This exercise and the two that follow present test programs that can be used to explore certain details of a BASIC interpreter. This first program is designed to reveal implementation-dependent features of input/ output statements. The Tab Test will show you how many tab stops your BASIC has, and how they are handled. The Semicolon Test shows whether or not spaces are placed between strings or numbers in output. The Input Test explores the prompts that are produced by the **INPUT** statement, with and without a prompt string. Run the program, and note the results. In particular, note which of the three **INPUT** and string-prompt statements (2, 3, or 4) is the best for your BASIC.*

```
10    PRINT "     INPUT/OUTPUT TESTS"
20    PRINT
30    PRINT "    1 ) TAB TEST"
40    PRINT "TAB1", "TAB2", "TAB3", "TAB4", "TAB5"
50    PRINT
60    PRINT "    2) SEMICOLON TEST"
70    PRINT "SPACES"; "OR"; "NO"; "SPACES"; "?"
80    PRINT 1; 2; 3; 4
90    PRINT
100   PRINT "    3) INPUT TESTS"
110   PRINT "1.  ";
120   INPUT X$
130   PRINT "2.  ";
140   INPUT "QUESTION"; X$
150   PRINT "3.  ";
160   INPUT "QUESTION?"; X$
170   PRINT "4.  ";
180   INPUT "QUESTION? "; X$
190   END
```

2.2: *This program explores the representations of "true" and "false" in BASIC. Study the program before you run it and make sure you understand what it does. Line 40 is difficult; remember that " = " has two different meanings in BASIC. Run the program. We will make use of what we learn from this program in Chapter 5.*

```
10  REM         BOOLEAN TEST
20  X = 1
30  Y = 2
40  F = X = Y : REM F IS ASSIGNED THE VALUE FALSE
50  T = NOT F : REM T IS ASSIGNED THE VALUE TRUE
60  PRINT "FALSE = "; F; " TRUE = "; T
70  END
```

2.3: *This last test program is designed to show you the range of real (or "floating-point") numbers in your BASIC. Note that there are two ways of writing real numbers in BASIC—decimal form, and exponent, or E-notation. The E followed by an integer indicates that the number is multiplied by 10 to the power of the integer. For example:*

```
1000  = 1E3
55000 = 5.5E4
.0003  = 3E−4
```

This program calculates and prints progressively smaller numbers (in an "infinite" loop) until the point is reached where BASIC can no longer represent the number. Note what happens when that point is reached; also make note of the smallest number your BASIC can represent.

```
10  REM         FLOATING−POINT TEST
20  REM         ADAPTED FROM PASCAL PROGRAMS FOR
30  REM         SCIENTISTS AND ENGINEERS
40  REM         BY ALAN R. MILLER
50  REM
60  X = 1.0E−4 / 3
70  PRINT "X = "; X
80  X = 0.1 * X
90  GOTO 70
```

Rewrite the program to explore the upper range of floating-point numbers.

CHAPTER 3

FOR Loops

IN THE LAST CHAPTER we saw how a group of instructions can be repeated any number of times by use of the **GOTO** statement. The **GOTO** creates a loop; in other words, control of the program is continually sent backward to the beginning of the set of instructions that are to be repeated.

Recall the following lines from the depreciation subroutine:

```
1120   PRINT "ORIGINAL COST OF ITEM #"; X%;
1130   INPUT C
       . . .
1310   INPUT "ANOTHER ITEM"; A$
1320   IF (A$ = "Y") OR (A$ = "YES") GOTO 1120
```

At the beginning of this loop the user inputs the original cost of a depreciable piece of equipment (line 1130). The item is processed in the body of the loop (lines 1140 to 1300), and finally the user is asked if there is another item to input (line 1310). If there is, the whole block of instructions is repeated (line 1320); if not, the next line (after 1320) is executed.

At the beginning of a **GOTO** loop we do not necessarily know how many times the instructions in the loop will be executed. The number of times, in this case, depends completely on the user's input.

BASIC provides the syntax for another kind of loop that is designed for cases where we do know (or can calculate) the number of times the loop will repeat. There are several ways to incorporate the number of repetitions into a program: it can be written explicitly into the loop instruction itself; it can be input by the user; or it can be calculated from other data. The control structure is called the **FOR** loop, and it is the subject of this chapter.

The main program of this chapter uses a **FOR** loop to produce a monthly sales report for a given number of months. The loop accumulates a running total for sales, and when the loop is finally finished, the program uses this total to compute the average monthly sales.

In this first version of our program we will see how simple and clear a **FOR** loop is. Once we have discussed this program, we will move one step further, to look at *nested* loops, or loops within loops. As an example of a nested loop, we will add instructions to our program to create a bar graph for the monthly sales report.

A Known Number of Repetitions

Looking once again at the depreciation subroutine, we can see that it would have been quite simple to ask the user for the number of depreciable items before the first run through the loop:

    1115   **INPUT** "HOW MANY DEPRECIABLE ITEMS"; I1%

Then, since the integer variable X% is already being used as a counter inside the loop (line 1140) lines 1300 and 1310 could have been replaced by:

    1310   **IF** (X% < = I1%) **GOTO** 1120

In other words, the block of instructions is repeated until X% exceeds the value of I1%, at which point the expression:

    X% < = I1%

is no longer true, and the line after 1310 will be executed.

The **FOR** loop is a much more elegant way to implement the same repetition structure. The syntax of the **FOR** loop is as follows:

    FOR I = A **TO** B **STEP** C

    . . .

    NEXT I

Let us outline the action of these statements:

1. I is first assigned the value A.

2. All the lines between the **FOR** statement and the **NEXT** statement are executed.

3. I is incremented by the value of C.

4. If, after the incrementation, I is still less than or equal to B, the statements within the loop are performed again (i.e., the sequence returns to step 2, above). Otherwise, if I is greater than B, execution of the loop ends.

5. After the last repetition of the loop, control passes to the statement following the **NEXT**.

Thus, we could write our depreciation loop as follows:

```
1115    INPUT "HOW MANY DEPRECIABLE ITEMS"; I1%
1117    FOR X% = 1 TO I1%
1120        PRINT "ORIGINAL COST OF ITEM #"; X%;
1130        INPUT C
        . . .
1310    NEXT X%
```

Notice that the **FOR** statement in line 1117 does not contain the word **STEP**. This is because the **STEP** instruction is optional; the *default value* of the incrementation of the **FOR** index is 1. That is to say, X% will be incremented by 1 for every repetition of the loop, unless **STEP** is used to specify another value.

Also, it is no longer necessary to increment X% "manually" with a statement such as:

```
1140    X% = X% + 1
```

This incrementation is performed automatically by the **FOR** loop.

There are two other important points to learn from the example above. First, it is a good idea to *indent* the lines that constitute the body of the loop (that is, all the lines between the **FOR** statement and the **NEXT** statement). This indentation makes the program easier to read; **FOR** loops can be easily distinguished from the rest of the program.

Second, notice that the variables in the **FOR** statement are all integers in this program. In fact, either integer or real variables are allowed in the **FOR** statement. (See Exercise 3.5.) Also, as we will see in a program in Chapter 6, the **STEP** instruction can be used to *decrement* the index, I, of the **FOR** loop if B < A and C is a negative number; for example:

FOR I = 25 **TO** 5 **STEP** −5

Producing a Sales Report

Let us say we wish to produce a report of the monthly unit sales for a certain period, and then find the average monthly sales for the entire period. We must begin, of course, by inputting the number of months in the period. This integer determines the number of times that the **FOR** loop in the program will be repeated:

INPUT "NUMBER OF MONTHS"; N%

The program, a very simple one, appears in Figure 3.1.

The **FOR** loop, in lines 60 to 90, contains two instructions. The first instruction is for the input of the month (M$) and the number of units sold during that month (U1). The second statement accumulates the total sales for the period:

80   U2 = U2 + U1

```
 10   PRINT "MONTHLY SALES STATISTICS"
 20   PRINT
 30   INPUT "NUMBER OF MONTHS"; N%
 40   PRINT "INPUT MONTH, NUMBER OF UNITS SOLD"
 50   U2 = 0
 60   FOR I% = 1 TO N%
 70      INPUT M$, U1
 80      U2 = U2 + U1
 90   NEXT I%
100   PRINT
110   PRINT "TOTAL UNITS SOLD IN "; N%; " MONTHS = "; U2
120   PRINT "AVERAGE NUMBER OF UNITS SOLD PER MONTH = "; INT(U2/N%)
130   END
```

Figure 3.1: First Version of Report on Monthly Sales

Notice that U2 is initialized to zero in line 50, just before the **FOR** loop.

Let us examine a flowchart for this short program (Figure 3.2). The flowchart contains an initialization statement for I% (I% = 1), an

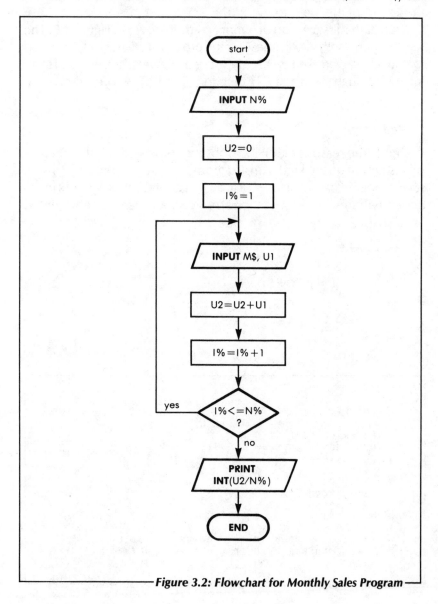

Figure 3.2: Flowchart for Monthly Sales Program

incrementation statement (I% = I% + 1), and a decision diamond (I% < N%?). None of these statements, however, appear explicitly in the program itself. All of them are performed by the **FOR/NEXT** loop. The last iteration of the loop is for I% = N%, after which control passes out of the loop, to the **PRINT** statement.

A run of this first version of our program is shown in Figure 3.3. The input of the month (M$ in line 70 of the program) creates a clear record for the sales report. The average number of units sold is truncated to an integer through use of the **INT** function (line 120) before it is printed.

Nested Loops

One of the reasons that **FOR** loops are so powerful is that there is no restriction on the kind of instructions that can be contained inside such a loop. In particular, a **FOR** loop can contain another **FOR** loop, *nested* within it. The syntax for a nested loop can be represented as follows:

FOR I = A **TO** B **STEP** C

. . .

FOR J = D **TO** E **STEP** F

. . .

NEXT J

. . .

NEXT I

```
MONTHLY SALES STATISTICS

NUMBER OF MONTHS? 6
INPUT MONTH, NUMBER OF UNITS SOLD
? JAN, 1567
? FEB, 1892
? MAR, 2319
? APR, 3450
? MAY, 2980
? JUN, 3120

TOTAL UNITS SOLD IN  6  MONTHS =   15328
AVERAGE NUMBER OF UNITS SOLD PER MONTH =   2554
```

Figure 3.3: Output from First Version of Sales Report Program

The inner loop (index J) is completely contained by the outer loop (index I); in other words, both **FOR** J and **NEXT** J occur between **FOR** I and **NEXT** I.

A classic exercise illustrating the action of nested loops is the multiplication table program of Figure 3.4. Its output, shown in Figure 3.5, is the sort of table that school children used to practice their multiplication factors before the advent of pocket calculators.

By examining the output, it is easy to see how this program works. The outer loop creates the ten rows; the inner loop prints ten numbers for each row. The inner loop goes through ten iterations for every iteration of the outer loop. For example, when I equals 3, J is incremented from 1 to 10, creating the row 3, 6, 9, . . . 30.

In the next section we will add a nested loop to our sales report

```
10   REM        MULTIPLICATION TABLE
20   REM        D. HERGERT        1 AUGUST 1981
30   REM
40   FOR I = 1 TO 10
50      FOR J = 1 TO 10
60         PRINT USING "####"; I * J;
70      NEXT J
80      PRINT
90   NEXT I
100  END
```

Figure 3.4: Multiplication Table Program

1	2	3	4	5	6	7	8	9	10
2	4	6	8	10	12	14	16	18	20
3	6	9	12	15	18	21	24	27	30
4	8	12	16	20	24	28	32	36	40
5	10	15	20	25	30	35	40	45	50
6	12	18	24	30	36	42	48	54	60
7	14	21	28	35	42	49	56	63	70
8	16	24	32	40	48	56	64	72	80
9	18	27	36	45	54	63	72	81	90
10	20	30	40	50	60	70	80	90	100

Figure 3.5: Output from Multiplication Table Program

program. The new loop will produce a horizontal bar graph; each bar of the graph will represent one month's sales.

Creating a Bar Graph

Two problems must be solved to add a bar graph to our report. First, we must decide on a character to use to create the bars of the graph. Second, we need a convenient way of determining how many units each character of the bar will represent.

Let us begin by using an X to build the bars. For a month in which 30 units have been sold, then, a bar of 30 Xs would represent the sales. We could create this bar using the value of U1, the input number of units sold:

```
FOR J% = 1 TO U1
    PRINT "X";
NEXT J%
```

This, then, is the form of the nested loop that we will add to our program to create the bar graph. For each iteration of the outer loop, a new value of U1 is input. The inner loop iterates U1 times, creating a line of "X" characters representing the number of sales.

The loop that we wrote above is fine for small numbers of units. However, when the number of units sold is larger, say 1000 to 5000, we would want each X to represent some quantity of units, say 100 in this case. Thus, there would be from 10 to 50 Xs in each bar, representing the sales *proportionally* rather than one-to-one.

We might simply prompt the user to input a scale factor for the bar graph. Then the number of Xs could be calculated from this scale factor:

```
INPUT "UNITS REPRESENTED BY ONE X"; U

. . .
FOR J% = 1 TO INT(U1/U)
    PRINT "X";
NEXT J%
```

The expression **INT**(U1/U) calculates the number of Xs that must be printed to produce a bar that is proportional in length to the sales for one month.

Finally, we can alter our program to allow different characters to be used to build the bar graph. If we add an **INPUT** line for the character, which we will store in the string variable C$, then we can alter our loop to print C$.

```
INPUT "FOR BAR GRAPH CHARACTER"; C$
PRINT "UNITS REPRESENTED BY ONE "; C$;
INPUT U

. . .

FOR J% = 1 TO INT(U1/U)
    PRINT C$
NEXT J%
```

The entire sales report program is listed in Figure 3.6; a sample run is given in Figure 3.7. Notice the **PRINT** statement on line 260. This performs a line feed at the end of each bar of the graph.

```
 10   REM      MONTHLY SALES STATISTICS WITH BAR GRAPH
 20   REM      D. HERGERT        25 JULY 1981
 30   REM
 40   REM      VARIABLE NAMES
 50   REM      N%                NUMBER OF MONTHS COVERED
 60   REM      C$                BAR GRAPH CHARACTER
 70   REM      U                 SCALE FACTOR FOR BAR GRAPH
 80   REM      U1                UNITS SOLD IN A GIVEN MONTH
 90   REM      U2                TOTAL UNITS SOLD DURING PERIOD
100   REM      M$                MONTH NAME
110   REM      I%, J%            LOOP INDICES
120   REM
130   PRINT "MONTHLY SALES STATISTICS"
140   PRINT
150   INPUT "NUMBER OF MONTHS"; N%
160   INPUT "BAR GRAPH CHARACTER"; C$
170   PRINT "UNITS REPRESENTED BY ONE "; C$;
180   INPUT U
190   PRINT "INPUT MONTH, NUMBER OF UNITS"
200   U2 = 0
```

Figure 3.6: Version Two of Sales Report Program

```
210    FOR I% = 1 TO N% : REM BEGINNING OF OUTER LOOP
220       INPUT M$, U1
230       FOR J% = 1 TO INT(U1/U) : REM BEGINNING OF INNER LOOP
240          PRINT C$;
250       NEXT J%
260       PRINT
270       U2 = U2 + U1 : REM INCREMENT TOTAL SALES
280    NEXT I%
290    PRINT
300    PRINT "TOTAL UNITS SOLD IN "; N%; " MONTHS = "; U2
310    PRINT "AVERAGE NUMBER OF UNITS SOLD PER MONTH = "; INT(U2/N%)
320    END
```

Figure 3.6: Version Two of Sales Report Program (cont.)

```
MONTHLY SALES STATISTICS

NUMBER OF MONTHS? 12
BAR GRAPH CHARACTER? X
UNITS REPRESENTED BY ONE X? 50
INPUT MONTH, NUMBER OF UNITS
? JAN, 1256
XXXXXXXXXXXXXXXXXXXXXXXXX
? FEB, 1476
XXXXXXXXXXXXXXXXXXXXXXXXXXXXX
? MAR, 2100
XXXXXXXXXXXXXXXXXXXXXXXXXXXXXXXXXXXXXXXXXX
? APR, 1940
XXXXXXXXXXXXXXXXXXXXXXXXXXXXXXXXXXXXXXX
? MAY, 2310
XXXXXXXXXXXXXXXXXXXXXXXXXXXXXXXXXXXXXXXXXXXXXX
? JUN, 2980
XXXXXXXXXXXXXXXXXXXXXXXXXXXXXXXXXXXXXXXXXXXXXXXXXXXXXXXXXXXXX
? JUL, 2547
XXXXXXXXXXXXXXXXXXXXXXXXXXXXXXXXXXXXXXXXXXXXXXXXXXX
? AUG, 2600
XXXXXXXXXXXXXXXXXXXXXXXXXXXXXXXXXXXXXXXXXXXXXXXXXXXX
? SEP, 2320
XXXXXXXXXXXXXXXXXXXXXXXXXXXXXXXXXXXXXXXXXXXXXX
? OCT, 1879
XXXXXXXXXXXXXXXXXXXXXXXXXXXXXXXXXXXXXX
? NOV, 2678
XXXXXXXXXXXXXXXXXXXXXXXXXXXXXXXXXXXXXXXXXXXXXXXXXXXXXX
? DEC, 2890
XXXXXXXXXXXXXXXXXXXXXXXXXXXXXXXXXXXXXXXXXXXXXXXXXXXXXXXXXXX

TOTAL UNITS SOLD IN  12 MONTHS =  26976
AVERAGE NUMBER OF UNITS SOLD PER MONTH =   2248
```

Figure 3.7: Output of Sales Report with Bar Graph

Figure 3.8 shows a flowchart for the nested loops of the sales report program. Again, notice the decisions, initializations, and incrementations that are actually performed by the **FOR/NEXT** loops.

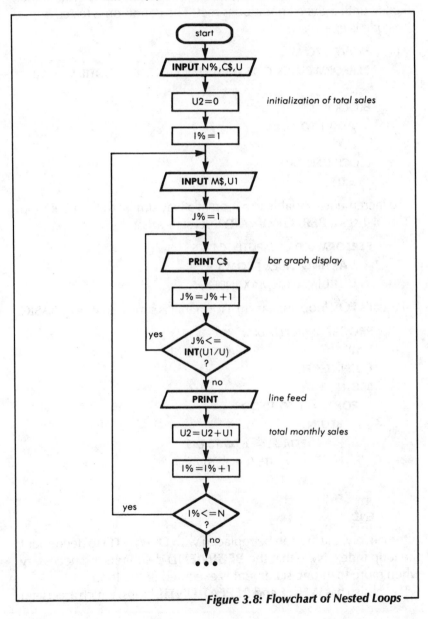

Figure 3.8: Flowchart of Nested Loops

Loops in Other Languages

COBOL implements loops through variations of the **PERFORM** statement. The **PERFORM/UNTIL** statement repeats a certain block of code until a given condition is met. The condition is tested *before* the code is executed:

```
MOVE 0 TO M.
PERFORM BLOCK-ONE THRU BLOCK-ONE-EXIT UNTIL M = 10.
. . .
BLOCK-ONE.
    ADD 1 TO M.
    . . .
BLOCK-ONE-EXIT.
    EXIT.
```

To increment a variable in a loop in a way similar to the **FOR** loop, COBOL uses a **PERFORM/VARYING** statement:

```
PERFORM 020-COMPUTE-TOTALS
    VARYING INDEX FROM 1 BY 1
    UNTIL INDEX > MAX-INDEX.
```

Pascal's **FOR** loop appears in a form that is similar to that of BASIC:

```
PROGRAM MULTTABLE;
VAR
I, J,: INTEGER;
BEGIN
    FOR I := 1 TO 10 DO
        BEGIN
            FOR J := 1 TO 10 DO
                WRITE (I * J : 5);
            WRITELN
        END
END.
```

Alternatively, the **TO** can be replaced with **DOWNTO** to decrement the loop index. Note that the **BEGIN/END** delimiters are necessary when more than one statement is executed in the loop.

Pascal also has **WHILE** and **REPEAT/UNTIL** loops, which are useful when the number of iterations is not known in advance. These loops can be used instead of **GOTO**s. Some BASICs also have a **WHILE/WEND** loop similar to the **WHILE** loop in Pascal.

In FORTRAN the **DO/CONTINUE** syntax is the equivalent of **FOR/NEXT**. The **CONTINUE** line must be numbered:

```
       DO 40 I = 1, 10
       DO 20 J = 1, 10
       K = I * J

         . . .

20     CONTINUE

         . . .

40     CONTINUE
```

Summary

FOR loops are useful when we know—or can calculate—the number of times a loop should be repeated. Nested loops are useful for varying more than one value in an intertwined series of iterations.

We will continue to examine the power of **FOR** loops in the chapters ahead. In particular, Chapter 4 will examine the combination of **FOR** loops and array data structures.

Exercises

3.1: *The following lines illustrate a technique of simulating the TAB function. Run the program, and explain what it does:*

```
10   PRINT TAB(20); "TAB(20)"
20   FOR I = 1 TO 20
30      PRINT " ";
40   NEXT I
50   PRINT "SIMULATED TAB(20)"
```

Now revise the program to simulate **TAB**$(X \wedge 2)$ *where X is an input value.*

3.2: *A useful addition to the monthly sales program (Figure 3.6) might be a "scale line" that would make it easy to read the length of each bar in the graph. The following routine produces such a line:*

```
10   C% = 64
20   FOR I% = 1 TO C%
30      IF I%/10 = INT(I%/10) GOTO 60
40      PRINT ".";
50      GOTO 70
60      PRINT "!";
70   NEXT I%
```

Run this routine to find out exactly what it does. Notice that line 50 ends one iteration of the loop by passing control to the **NEXT** *statement. What does line 30 do? Renumber this routine and put it in the monthly sales program at an appropriate place.*

*3.3: *To make the bar graph clearer or more dramatic, we might want to double the thickness of each bar by printing two lines of characters instead of only one. This could be done by increasing the level of nested loops in the program to three. Revise the monthly sales report program to produce this effect. (Hint: use* **FOR** K% = 1 **TO** 2 *as the middle loop.)*

3.4: *BASIC allows us to "jump out" of a loop before the loop has completed all of its iterations; however, in some circumstances (and in some versions of BASIC) this may lead to trouble if the index of the loop that was prematurely ended is used again elsewhere in the program. The following test program is designed to reveal how any* *version of BASIC will react in these special circumstances. The first loop, with index I%, is terminated when I% equals 9. The index I% is used again in a nested loop later in the program. Run this program and note the results.*

```
10   REM        NEXT WITHOUT FOR LOOP
20   REM        ADAPTED FROM BASIC PROGRAMS FOR
25   REM               SCIENTISTS AND ENGINEERS
30   REM        BY ALAN R. MILLER
40   REM
50   REM        FIRST LOOP — — TERMINATED WHEN I% = 9
60   FOR I% = 1 TO 10
70     IF I% = 9 THEN 90
80   NEXT I%
90   PRINT "*** LINE 90:  I% = "; I%
100  REM        NESTED LOOPS — — INNER LOOP USES I%
110  FOR J% = 1 TO 2
120    FOR I% = 1 TO 10
130      PRINT J%; ": "; I%
140    NEXT I%
150  NEXT J%
160  END
```

3.5: *Experiment with the **STEP** instruction by writing **FOR** loops that will produce:*

a) *a list of positive numbers from 1 to 10 in increments of 0.1;*
b) *a list of negative numbers from 0 to −10 in increments of −0.1.*

*3.6: *Revise the monthly sales program to produce a bar for cash sales and credit sales for each month of the report. Use different graphics characters to represent each category of sales.*

---

*Answer appears in Appendix A.

CHAPTER 4

Arrays

UP TO THIS POINT we have worked with variables that can be assigned only one value at a time. If we give a value to the variable V:

    100   V = 5.72

and then change that value later in the program:

    110   V = V * I

then the original value of V is lost. If we had wanted to save the original value, we might have assigned it to another variable before statement 110:

    105   U = V

This method of saving related data is adequate when we are working with only a few values. Many times in programming, however, we find ourselves with sets of related data that we would like to store together in a convenient way. Hundreds of values might be involved, so we would not want to use a different variable for each value. We need a way of storing all of these values under one name, and a way of *accessing* any one value whenever we need it.

The structure that we use in programming to store multiple values in one variable is the *array*. Array elements are sometimes called *subscripted variables* because they are referred to in a way that corresponds to the mathematical notation of subscripts. For example, in subscript notation we might write the projected yearly income of a company for the next five years as follows:

$$I_1 = 13{,}000$$
$$I_2 = 20{,}000$$
$$I_3 = 29{,}000$$
$$I_4 = 40{,}000$$
$$I_5 = 55{,}000$$

The I tells us that this is the variable that holds the income. The subscript tells us which year's income we are dealing with.

As we will see, the BASIC equivalent of these statements is:

```
I(1) = 13000
I(2) = 20000
I(3) = 29000
I(4) = 40000
I(5) = 55000
```

These statements assign values to five elements of the one-dimensional array I.

In this chapter we will explore the use of arrays in BASIC. The major program of the chapter computes the present value of a depreciation under different depreciation methods. We will first see how to produce the present value tables using BASIC. Then, as we continue to work our way through the depreciation program, we will see how a potentially complicated problem is greatly simplified by the use of arrays.

In the first part of this chapter we will use only one-dimensional arrays. Toward the end of the chapter, however, we will discuss arrays of more than one dimension. We will see how to use multi-dimensional arrays with nested **FOR** loops to form a tremendously powerful programming tool.

The Present Value Tables

To account for the time-value of money when comparing the future returns of different investments, we compute the *net present value* of the investments. The discount and annuity factors used to compute the present value for up to twenty years are tabulated in Figures 4.1 and 4.2, respectively. The column headings represent interest rates (or what we will be calling the "expected rate of return on investment"), and the rows are the number of years of investment. Let us review briefly the use and formulation of these tables.

The present value of a future inflow or outflow of a sum of money is determined by multiplying the sum of money by the appropriate present value discount factor in Figure 4.1.

For example, let us consider an investment that will return $5,000 in five years. At a 6% rate of return, what is the present value of the investment? We see that the discount factor for five years at 6% is 0.747; therefore, the present value of the investment is:

$$\$5,000 \times 0.747 = \$3,735$$

	4%	6%	8%	10%	12%	14%	16%	18%	20%
1	0.962	0.943	0.926	0.909	0.893	0.877	0.862	0.847	0.833
2	0.925	0.890	0.857	0.826	0.797	0.769	0.743	0.718	0.694
3	0.889	0.840	0.794	0.751	0.712	0.675	0.641	0.609	0.579
4	0.855	0.792	0.735	0.683	0.636	0.592	0.552	0.516	0.482
5	0.822	0.747	0.681	0.621	0.567	0.519	0.476	0.437	0.402
6	0.790	0.705	0.630	0.564	0.507	0.456	0.410	0.370	0.335
7	0.760	0.665	0.583	0.513	0.452	0.400	0.354	0.314	0.279
8	0.731	0.627	0.540	0.467	0.404	0.351	0.305	0.266	0.233
9	0.703	0.592	0.500	0.424	0.361	0.308	0.263	0.225	0.194
10	0.676	0.558	0.463	0.386	0.322	0.270	0.227	0.191	0.162
11	0.650	0.527	0.429	0.350	0.287	0.237	0.195	0.162	0.135
12	0.625	0.497	0.397	0.319	0.257	0.208	0.168	0.137	0.112
13	0.601	0.469	0.368	0.290	0.229	0.182	0.145	0.116	0.093
14	0.577	0.442	0.340	0.263	0.205	0.160	0.125	0.099	0.078
15	0.555	0.417	0.315	0.239	0.183	0.140	0.108	0.084	0.065
16	0.534	0.394	0.292	0.218	0.163	0.123	0.093	0.071	0.054
17	0.513	0.371	0.270	0.198	0.146	0.108	0.080	0.060	0.045
18	0.494	0.350	0.250	0.180	0.130	0.095	0.069	0.051	0.038
19	0.475	0.331	0.232	0.164	0.116	0.083	0.060	0.043	0.031
20	0.456	0.312	0.215	0.149	0.104	0.073	0.051	0.037	0.026

Figure 4.1: Present Value Discount Factors

On the other hand, if the investment will return $1,000 per year for the next five years, we would use the annuity factor (4.212 from Figure 4.2) to calculate the present value:

$$\$1,000 \times 4.212 = \$4,212$$

The formula for calculating the present value factors listed in Figure 4.1 is:

$$D = \frac{1}{(1 + r)^n} \tag{1}$$

where r is the expected rate of return (expressed as a decimal) and n is the number of years of investment.

	4%	6%	8%	10%	12%	14%	16%	18%	20%
1	0.962	0.943	0.926	0.909	0.893	0.877	0.862	0.847	0.833
2	1.886	1.833	1.783	1.736	1.690	1.647	1.605	1.566	1.528
3	2.775	2.673	2.577	2.487	2.402	2.322	2.246	2.174	2.106
4	3.630	3.465	3.312	3.170	3.037	2.914	2.798	2.690	2.589
5	4.452	4.212	3.993	3.791	3.605	3.433	3.274	3.127	2.991
6	5.242	4.917	4.623	4.355	4.111	3.889	3.685	3.498	3.326
7	6.002	5.582	5.206	4.868	4.564	4.288	4.039	3.812	3.605
8	6.733	6.210	5.747	5.335	4.968	4.639	4.344	4.078	3.837
9	7.435	6.802	6.247	5.759	5.328	4.946	4.607	4.303	4.031
10	8.111	7.360	6.710	6.145	5.650	5.216	4.833	4.494	4.192
11	8.760	7.887	7.139	6.495	5.938	5.453	5.029	4.656	4.327
12	9.385	8.384	7.536	6.814	6.194	5.660	5.197	4.793	4.439
13	9.986	8.853	7.904	7.103	6.424	5.842	5.342	4.910	4.533
14	10.563	9.295	8.244	7.367	6.628	6.002	5.468	5.008	4.611
15	11.118	9.712	8.559	7.606	6.811	6.142	5.575	5.092	4.675
16	11.652	10.106	8.851	7.824	6.974	6.265	5.669	5.162	4.730
17	12.166	10.477	9.122	8.022	7.120	6.373	5.749	5.222	4.775
18	12.659	10.828	9.372	8.201	7.250	6.467	5.818	5.273	4.812
19	13.134	11.158	9.604	8.365	7.366	6.550	5.877	5.316	4.844
20	13.590	11.470	9.818	8.514	7.469	6.623	5.929	5.353	4.870

Figure 4.2: Annuity Factors

The relationship between Figures 4.1 and 4.2 is easy to understand. Each value of Figure 4.2 is the sum of the corresponding column of values in Figure 4.1. For example, the annuity factor for a 6% five-year investment is:

$$
\begin{array}{r}
0.943 \\
0.890 \\
0.840 \\
0.792 \\
+0.747 \\
\hline
4.212
\end{array}
$$

We could also derive a formula for computing the annuity factor (see Exercise 4.6), but in our BASIC program we will be calculating this factor as a sum of a column of present value discount factors.

A BASIC Program for Discount Factors

Equation 1 can easily be written as a BASIC expression:

```
10    D = 1 / ((1 + R)^N)
```

(Remember that the raised caret(^) symbol represents exponentiation in BASIC.) We might revise the statement slightly to allow input of a percent rather than a decimal for R:

```
10    D = 1 / ((1 + R/100)^N
```

We can incorporate this statement into a short program that accepts an interest rate and a number of years as input and gives the discount factor as output:

```
 5    INPUT "RATE (%), YEARS";R,N
10    D = 1/((1 + R/100)^N)
15    PRINT "DISCOUNT FACTOR = "; D
20    END
```

Writing a program to compute the annuity factor is slightly more complicated. The flowchart in Figure 4.3 describes the algorithm. Again, the program begins by prompting the user to input the interest rate and the number of years of investment. Then the annuity factor A is initialized to zero. The program next begins a loop that calculates each discount factor for the years 1 to N and sums up the factors in the variable A. This is the same as adding up a column of values in Figure 4.1 to arrive at a value in Figure 4.2. The program, again a short one, looks like this:

```
5    INPUT "RATE (%), YEARS";R, N
10   A = 0
15   FOR I = 1 TO N
20      D = 1/((1 + R/100)^I)
25      A = A + D
30   NEXT I
35   PRINT "ANNUITY FACTOR = "; A
40   END
```

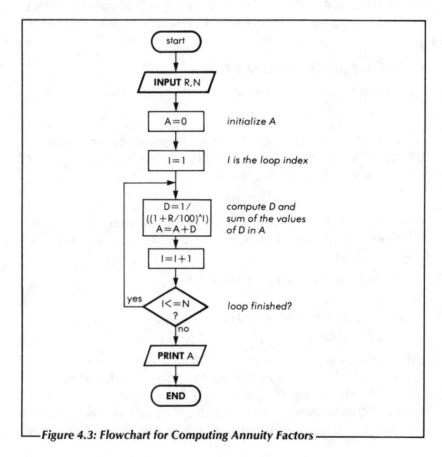

Figure 4.3: Flowchart for Computing Annuity Factors

The one difficulty of this program is that the intermediate values of D that are added up to arrive at the final value of A are lost. Of course, we could include a **PRINT** statement inside the loop to print a record of each value of D before it is lost:

   22   **PRINT** D

But what if we needed to *use* the values of D in another part of a longer program?

The solution to this problem, of course, is to make D an *array*. Before we revise this program, however, let us examine the use of arrays in BASIC.

Arrays

BASIC gives us a statement for defining an array and a way of referencing each element of an array. We will study each of these features in turn.

The **DIM** statement (for *dim*ension) is used to set up an array. Writing this statement requires three pieces of information:

1. the name of the array
2. the number of dimensions in the array
3. the number of elements (or the *length*) of each dimension.

The general form of the **DIM** statement is:

   DIM V1(N1,N2, . . .), V2(M1,M2, . . .), . . .

where V1, V2, . . . are variable names, and N1, N2, M1, and M2 are integers representing the length of each dimension. For the moment we will be working with one-dimensional arrays only, so we can abbreviate this format to:

   DIM V1(N), V2(M), . . .

Notice that one **DIM** statement can define more than one array. A program can, however, have more than one **DIM** statement, so that an alternative form is:

   DIM V1(N)
   DIM V2(N)

   . . .

The maximum length allowed for each dimension of an array varies for different versions of BASIC.

One last note on the **DIM** statement: If a programmer fails to include such a statement in a program and then uses an array anyway, the default value for the length of that array is 11 in most BASICs. That is, the array will contain elements 0 to 10. There will be no problem as long as no reference is made to A(11) or beyond. If A(11) *is* referenced, the program will end prematurely with an error message. It is safer and clearer, therefore, to include a **DIM** statement for all the arrays in a program.

References to one-dimensional array elements take the following form in BASIC:

V(N)

where V is the name of a variable defined in a **DIM** statement, and N refers to the Nth element of that array (actually, (N + 1)th if we count the zeroth element). N can be an integer, a variable, or an expression. Thus, all of the following are legal:

A(5)   A(K)
A(I+K)   A(I/K)
A(I−K)   A(I^2)

If N turns out to be a positive noninteger value, it will simply be truncated. If N is negative, however, the program will end with an error message.

In BASICs that have variable typing, arrays can be typed just as other variables can. For example:

DIM Q(30), P$(30), R%(30)

defines three one-dimensional arrays. Q is an array of real numbers, P$ is an array of strings, and R% is an array of integers. All the elements of an array must hold the same type of value. Thus:

Q(30) = 1.532
P$(19) = "HELLO THERE"
R%(27) = 29

are all legal, but:

P$(27) = 1.24

is not.

Now that we have studied the syntax of arrays in BASIC, we are ready to return to the annuity program. We will eventually rewrite this program for use in a longer program that we will begin planning a little later in the chapter. We will also write two other routines, both illustrating interesting uses of arrays.

The Improved Annuity Program

We only need to make a few changes in the annuity program in order to store the discount factors in an array. First, we will write a **DIM** statement; let us say we wish to calculate discount factors for up to 30 years:

3   **DIM** D(30)

Then we will change variable D to an array in lines 20 and 25:

20   D(I) = 1 / ((1 + R/100)^I)
25   A = A + D(I)

Finally we can add a **PRINT** statement for the values of D if we wish:

23   **PRINT TAB**(18); D(I)

We have already seen that we could have included a similar **PRINT** statement in the earlier program, where D was a simple variable. The difference here is that we are not only *printing* the values of D; we are also saving them in the program itself so we can use them again if we need them.

Figure 4.4 shows the entire annuity program and Figure 4.5 shows a sample run. Notice the relationship between the **FOR** loop and the array. The loop index I references the array element D(I) and is also part of the right side of the assignment statement in line 20. We begin to see how powerful and elegant a tool we now have at our disposal.

The loop continues to increment I until N elements of the array D have been assigned values. We can access those values any time by referring to D(1), D(2), and so on. Or we can refer to D(M), where M is an integer within the defined length of the array D. (Note that we do *not* have to use I again to reference elements of D. The variable I was simply the most convenient one to use for assigning values to D inside the **FOR** loop.)

We will soon be using a version of the annuity program again as a

```
1    REM        PRESENT VALUE FACTORS
2    REM
3    DIM D(30)
5    INPUT "INTEREST RATE (PERCENT), NUMBER OF YEARS (30 MAXIMUM)"; R, N
10   A = 0
15   FOR I = 1 TO N
20       D(I) = 1 / ((1 + R/100)^I)
23       PRINT TAB(18); D(I)
25       A = A + D(I)
30   NEXT I
35   PRINT "ANNUITY FACTOR = "; A
40   END
```

Figure 4.4: The Annuity Program

```
INTEREST RATE (PERCENT), NUMBER OF YEARS (30 MAXIMUM)? 18, 10
                  .847458
                  .718184
                  .608631
                  .515789
                  .437109
                  .370432
                  .313925
                  .266038
                  .225456
                  .191064
ANNUITY FACTOR =  4.49409
```

Figure 4.5: Sample Run of Annuity Program

subroutine in the major program of this chapter. Recall that we saw our first example of a subroutine in the COGS program of Chapter 1. A subroutine is a group of statements that are accessed via a **GOSUB** statement. For example, the statement:

GOSUB 2000

sends control of the program to line 2000. The lines from 2000 on are then executed sequentially until the statement:

RETURN

appears. The **RETURN** sends control of the program back to the line following the same **GOSUB** statement that was used to "call" the subroutine. We will be discussing subroutines and program structure in detail in Chapter 5. In the main program of this chapter we will simply use subroutines to isolate several important parts of our program. The present value subroutine appears in Figure 4.6.

Note that this subroutine does not have a **DIM** statement. The array D will be dimensioned, along with some other arrays, in a **DIM** statement at the beginning of the main program.

```
2000  REM      PRESENT VALUE SUBROUTINE
2001  REM
2002  REM      VARIABLE NAMES
2003  REM      D              ARRAY OF PRESENT VALUE FACTORS
2004  REM      N              NUMBER OF YEARS INVESTMENT
2005  REM      A              ANNUITY FACTOR FOR N YEARS
2006  REM      R              EXPECTED RATE OF RETURN (PERCENT)
2007  REM
2010  A = 0
2020  FOR I = 1 TO N
2030      D(I) = 1 / (1 + R/100)^I
2040      A = A + D(I)
2050  NEXT I
2060  RETURN
```

Figure 4.6: Present Value Subroutine

A First Look at the Depreciation Program

Before we go on to look at some more examples of arrays, we should take a look at the complete program we will be building. The program calculates the present value of a depreciation. Since depreciation expense is deducted from income, it "shields" a known amount of income from taxation over the useful life of the asset being depreciated. Thus, we can compute the present value of the income that is shielded. The present value will vary under different depreciation methods. Our program will calculate the present value of a depreciation under three methods commonly used in the United States today:

1. straight-line depreciation

2. sum-of-the-years'-digits (SYD) depreciation

3. double-declining-balance (DDB) depreciation

(We will assume a residual value of zero in this program; see Exercise 4.5 for information on residual values.)

Straight-line depreciation can be considered an annuity because an equal amount is depreciated each year of the useful life of the asset. For example, a $50,000 piece of equipment with a useful life of ten years will be depreciated at $5,000 per year under the straight-line method. If the tax rate is 50%, then the yearly tax savings is $2,500, which can be thought of as a ten-year $2,500 annuity.

The sum-of-the-years'-digits and double-declining-balance methods, on the other hand, are *accelerated* depreciation methods, which allow larger sums to be depreciated during the early years of the useful life of the asset than in the later years. As our program will show, the present value of the depreciation (that is, the present value of the projected tax savings) is greater under accelerated methods than under the straight-line method.

Figure 4.7 shows a flowchart for the program we will be writing. So far we have written the subroutine for calculating the present value discount factors (which we will use for the present value of the accelerated depreciation methods) and the annuity factor (which we will use for the straight-line method). In the next section we will write the subroutines for computing the two accelerated depreciation methods themselves—SYD and DDB.

More Array Examples

The algorithm for the sum-of-the-years'-digits depreciation method can be expressed as:

$$S_i = \frac{Y_i}{Y}C \qquad (2)$$

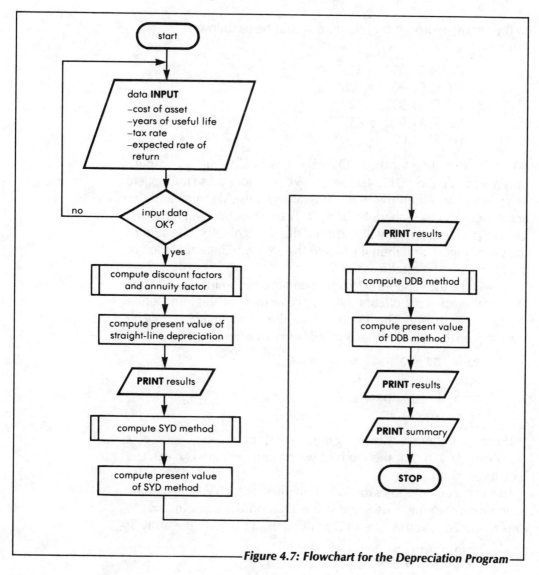

Figure 4.7: Flowchart for the Depreciation Program

where Y_i is the asset's *remaining* number of useful years (at the beginning of year i), Y is the "sum of the years' digits," and C is the acquisition cost of the asset.

For example, consider a piece of equipment that costs $1,000 and has a five-year useful life. The denominator, Y, is:

$$5 + 4 + 3 + 2 + 1 = 15$$

so the yearly depreciation schedule would be as follows:

Year
1 (5/15) $1,000 = $333
2 (4/15) $1,000 =   267
3 (3/15) $1,000 =   200
4 (2/15) $1,000 =   133
5 (1/15) $1,000 =   67

In our subroutine for the SYD method, we will actually compute only the multipliers (5/15, 4/15, etc.). We will store these multipliers in an array, and then the main program will use them to find the actual depreciation schedule for SYD. The subroutine will have two tasks to perform. First it will compute the denominator (the sum of the years' digits), and then it will find the SYD multiplier for each of the N years of the asset's useful life.

We will use the variable D2 to represent the denominator and N for the number of years of useful life. A flowchart for this subroutine appears in Figure 4.8. The first loop finds the denominator simply by summing up the values of the loop index I as it increments from 1 to N:

```
3010   D2 = 0
3020   FOR I = 1 TO N
3030     D2 = D2 + I
3040   NEXT I
```

There is another way of finding the sum of the consecutive integers (see Exercise 4.3), but the method we have used here is clear and easy to program.

The next loop computes the SYD multiplier for each year. Its central assignment statement uses the value D2 and the loop index I to implement Equation 2. The SYD multipliers are held in the array S:

```
3070   S(I) = (N - (I - 1)) / D2
```

Notice that the numerator of the multiplier decreases as the index I increases. Since this line is a little confusing, we will simplify it by creating another variable, X1, which will have a value of one less than I. The entire subroutine appears in Figure 4.9.

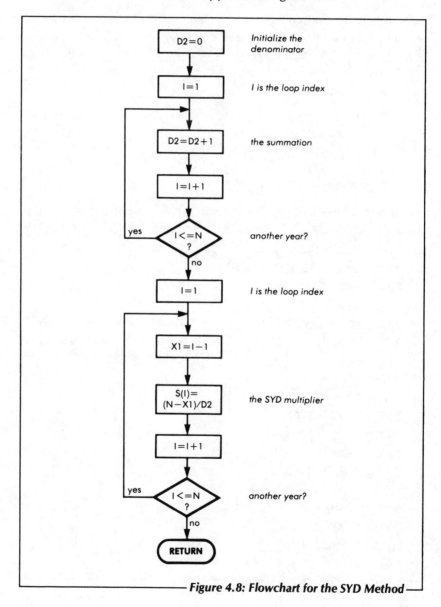

Figure 4.8: Flowchart for the SYD Method

The DDB algorithm is simply:

$$B_i = \frac{2C_i}{n}$$ (3)

where C_i is the remaining undepreciated cost of the asset at year i, and n is the total useful life of the asset. Thus, for our $1,000 asset with a five-year useful life, the DDB depreciation schedule would be as follows:

Year
1 (2 × $1000)/5 = $400
2 (2 × $600)/5 = 240
3 (2 × $360)/5 = 140
4 (2 × $220)/5 =   88
5 $1000 − 868 = 132

Notice that the last year's depreciation is simply the remaining undepreciated cost. The last year's depreciation often ends up being

```
3000  REM      SYD SUBROUTINE
3001  REM
3002  REM      VARIABLE NAMES
3003  REM      D2                  DENOMINATOR OF SYD FACTORS
3004  REM      N                   NUMBER OF YEARS USEFUL LIFE
3005  REM      S                   ARRAY OF SYD FACTORS
3006  REM
3010  D2 = 0
3020  FOR I = 1 TO N
3030     D2 = D2 + I
3040  NEXT I
3050  FOR I = 1 TO N
3060     X1 = I − 1
3070     S(I) = (N − X1)/D2
3080  NEXT I
3090  RETURN
```

Figure 4.9: SYD Subroutine

more than the next-to-last year's depreciation under DDB. For this reason, some companies will switch to SYD during the final years of the depreciation period (see Exercise 4.4).

The DDB subroutine is shown in Figure 4.10. Line 4030 computes all but the last year's depreciation, and stores the values in array B. Line 4040 sums up the total depreciated cost and, outside the loop, line 4060 computes the last year's depreciation, B(N).

We have now written the three important subroutines that we will need for our tax shield program. Each of them creates an array of values that will be used in the main program. Array D contains the present value discount factors. (The variable A is the summation of the values in D—that is, the annuity factor.) Array S contains the SYD multipliers. Array B contains the DDB yearly depreciation values. Predictably, the first line of our program (after the **REM** lines that supply a list of variable names) will define these three one-dimensional arrays:

> **DIM** D(30), S(30), B(30)

Since each array is defined with a length of 30, we will have to limit

```
4000   REM      DDB SUBROUTINE
4001   REM
4002   REM      VARIABLE NAMES
4003   REM      B2              AMOUNT ALREADY DEPRECIATED
4004   REM      C               ORIGINAL COST OF EQUIPMENT
4005   REM      N               NUMBER OF YEARS USEFUL LIFE
4006   REM      B               ARRAY OF DDB DEPRECIATION VALUES
4007   REM
4010   B2 = 0
4020   FOR I = 1 TO N − 1
4030       B(I) = (2 * (C − B2))/N
4040       B2 = B2 + B(I)
4050   NEXT I
4060   B(N) = C − B2
4070   RETURN
```

Figure 4.10: DDB Subroutine

the number of years of useful life to 30. (Actually, the arrays could hold 31 values, but our program works from year 1 to year N, so we will still not use D(0), S(0), or B(0).)

In the next section we will take a look at the program we have been building.

The Present Value of a Depreciation

The listing of the main program is shown in Figure 4.11. The three subroutines that we have already seen are simply identified by their first **REM** lines; they must, of course, be included in the program before execution. A sample run is shown in Figure 4.12. The program is long, but notice that many of the lines are devoted to printing headings. In fact, the subroutine at line 1000 is called twice—to print headings for both the SYD and the DDB methods.

The main program can be divided into five parts. The input section (lines 20 to 120) asks the user for the required data: the cost of the asset, the useful life, the tax rate, and the expected rate of return on investment. Each input value is tested to make sure it falls within the range of acceptable values. The next three sections compute and print the present value of the depreciation tax shield for each of the methods we have discussed: straight-line (lines 130 to 290), SYD (lines 300 to 460), and DDB (lines 470 to 610). Finally, the last section prints a comparison summary of the three methods if the user so requests (lines 620 to 750).

Notice that the BASIC command **CLS** is used to clear the screen between the different portions of the output (lines 330, 500, and 640). Some versions of BASIC use **HOME** in place of **CLS**.

```
1   REM     DEPRECIATION PROGRAM
2   REM     D. HERGERT        1 MAY 1981
3   REM
4   REM     VARIABLE NAMES
5   REM     D                 ARRAY OF PRESENT VALUE FACTORS
6   REM     A                 ANNUITY FACTOR FOR N YEARS
7   REM     S                 ARRAY OF SYD FACTORS
```

Figure 4.11: Present Value of a Depreciation

```
  8  REM       B                        ARRAY OF DDB DEPRECIATION VALUES
  9  REM
 10  DIM D(30), S(30), B(30)
 20  PRINT TAB(10); "AFTER—TAX EFFECTS OF DEPRECIATION"
 30  PRINT : PRINT
 40  INPUT "COST OF ASSET (LESS THAN 1 MILLION)"; C
 50  IF C > 999999 GOTO 40
 60  INPUT "NUMBER OF YEARS USEFUL LIFE (NOT MORE THAN 30)"; N
 70  IF N > 30 GOTO 60
 80  INPUT "TAX RATE (PERCENT)"; T1
 90  IF T1 > = 100 GOTO 80
100  INPUT "EXPECTED RATE OF RETURN ON INVESTMENT (PERCENT)"; R
110  IF R > = 100 GOTO 100
120  PRINT : PRINT
130  GOSUB 2000 : REM COMPUTE PRESENT VALUE FACTORS
140  PRINT TAB(10); "STRAIGHT—LINE DEPRECIATION" : REM HEADING
150  PRINT
160  PRINT , "TOTAL" ,, "DISCOUNT"
170  PRINT "ANNUAL", "SAVINGS", "YEARLY", "FACTOR—"
180  PRINT "DEPREC—", "AT ";T1;"%", "SAVINGS", "PRESENT"
190  PRINT "IATION", "INCOME",, "VALUE OF"
200  PRINT , "TAX" ,, "ANNUITY"
210  PRINT "— — — — — —", "— — — — — —", "— — — — — —", "— — — — — —"
220  PRINT
223  REM
225  REM        STRAIGHT—LINE DEPRECIATION CALCULATION
227  REM
230  S1 = C / N : REM ANNUAL DEPRECIATION
240  S2 = C * T1 / 100 : REM TOTAL TAX SAVINGS
250  S3 = S2 / N : REM YEARLY TAX SAVINGS
260  S4 = S3 * A : REM PRESENT VALUE OF TAX SAVINGS
270  X$ = "$$#####.##   $$#####.##   $$#####.##    ##.##"
280  PRINT USING X$; S1, S2, S3, A
```

Figure 4.11: Present Value of a Depreciation (cont.)

```
290   PRINT USING "TOTAL PRESENT VALUE = $$#####.##"; S4 : PRINT
300   GOSUB 3000 : REM COMPUTE SYD FACTORS
310   INPUT "READY FOR SUM−OF−THE−YEARS−DIGITS METHOD"; R1$
320   IF (R1$ <> "Y") AND ("R1$ <> "YES"") GOTO 310
330   CLS : REM CLEAR SCREEN
340   PRINT TAB(10); "SUM−OF−THE−YEARS'−DIGITS DEPRECIATION"
350   GOSUB 1000 : REM PRINT HEADING
360   Y4 = 0
370   W$ = "## $$#####.## $$#####.##    .###    $$#####.##"
373   REM
375   REM       SYD CALCULATION
377   REM
380   FOR I = 1 TO N
390      Y1 = C * S(I) : REM DEPRECIATION FOR YEAR I
400      Y2 = Y1 * T1/100 : REM TAX SAVINGS, YEAR I
410      Y3 = Y2 * D(I) : REM PRESENT VAL OF TAX SAVINGS
420      Y4 = Y4 + Y3 : REM TOTAL PRESENT VALUE
430      PRINT USING W$; I, Y1, Y2, D(I), Y3
440   NEXT I
450   PRINT USING "TOTAL PRESENT VALUE = $$#####.##"; Y4
460   PRINT
470   GOSUB 4000 : REM CALCULATE DDB VALUES
480   INPUT "READY FOR DOUBLE−DECLINING−BALANCE METHOD"; R2$
490   IF (R2$ <> "Y") AND (R2$ <> "YES") GOTO 480
500   CLS : REM CLEAR SCREEN
510   PRINT TAB(10); "DOUBLE−DECLINING−BALANCE DEPRECIATION"
520   GOSUB 1000 : REM PRINT HEADINGS
530   B3 = 0
540   FOR I = 1 TO N
550      B1 = B(I) * T1/100 : REM TAX SAVINGS, YEAR I
560      B2 = B1 * D(I) : REM PRESENT VAL OF TAX SAVINGS
570      B3 = B3 + B2 : REM TOTAL PRESENT VALUE
580      PRINT USING W$; I, B(I), B1, D(I), B2
590   NEXT I
```

Figure 4.11: Present Value of a Depreciation (cont.)

```
600   PRINT USING "TOTAL PRESENT VALUE = $$#####.##"; B3
610   PRINT
620   INPUT "DO YOU WANT A SUMMARY"; R3$
630   IF (R3$ = "N") OR (R3$ = "NO") STOP
640   CLS : REM CLEAR SCREEN
650   PRINT "SUMMARY — —AFTER TAX EFFECTS OF DEPRECIATION"
660   PRINT
670   PRINT "COST OF ASSET = $"; C
680   PRINT "USEFUL LIFE = "; N; "YEARS"
690   PRINT "TAX RATE = "; TX; "%"
700   PRINT "EXPECTED RATE OF RETURN ON INVESTMENT = "; R; "%"
710   PRINT
720   Q1$ = "PRESENT VAL UNDER STRAIGHT LINE DEPREC = $$#####.##"
725   PRINT USING Q1$; S4
730   Q2$ = "PRESENT VAL UNDER SYD DEPREC = $$#####.##"
735   PRINT USING Q2$; Y4
740   Q3$ = "PRESENT VAL UNDER DDB DEPREC = $$#####.##"
745   PRINT USING Q3$; B3
750   PRINT
760   STOP
1000  PRINT
1010  PRINT , "  INCOME", "PRESENT"
1020  PRINT , "  TAX", " VALUE"
1030  PRINT "    DEPREC—" , "  SAVINGS", "DISCOUNT", "PRESENT"
1040  PRINT "YEAR  IATION", "  AT "; T1;"%", "FACTOR"," VALUE"
1050  PRINT "_ _ _ _ _ _ _ _ _ _", "  _ _ _ _ _ _ _", "_ _ _ _ _ _" , "_ _ _ _ _"
1060  RETURN

2000  REM      PRESENT VALUE SUBROUTINE
2001  REM      FIGURE 4.6

3000  REM      SYD SUBROUTINE
3001  REM      FIGURE 4.9

4000  REM      DDB SUBROUTINE
4001  REM      FIGURE 4.10
```

Figure 4.11: Present Value of a Depreciation (cont.)

```
              AFTER-TAX EFFECTS OF DEPRECIATION


COST OF ASSET (LESS THAN 1 MILLION)? 230000
NUMBER OF YEARS USEFUL LIFE (NOT MORE THAN 30)? 8
TAX RATE (PERCENT)? 35
EXPECTED RATE OF RETURN ON INVESTMENT (PERCENT)? 18


              STRAIGHT-LINE DEPRECIATION

                    TOTAL                             DISCOUNT
ANNUAL              SAVINGS          YEARLY            FACTOR--
DEPREC-             AT 35 %          SAVINGS           PRESENT
IATION              INCOME                             VALUE OF
                    TAX                                ANNUITY
------              ------           ------            ------

 $28750.00        $80500.00        $10062.50          4.08


TOTAL PRESENT VALUE =    $41030.50

READY FOR SUM-OF-THE-YEARS-DIGITS METHOD? Y





              SUM-OF-THE-YEARS-DIGITS DEPRECIATION

                    INCOME           PRESENT
                    TAX              VALUE
          DEPREC-   SAVINGS          DISCOUNT          PRESENT
YEAR      IATION    AT 35 %          FACTOR            VALUE
----      ------    -------          ------            -----
 1      $51111.10   $17888.90        .847            $15160.10
 2      $44722.20   $15652.80        .718            $11241.60
 3      $38333.30   $13416.70        .609             $8165.80
 4      $31944.40   $11180.60        .516             $5766.81
 5      $25555.60    $8944.45        .437             $3909.70
 6      $19166.70    $6708.33        .370             $2484.98
 7      $12777.80    $4472.22        .314             $1403.94
 8       $6388.89    $2236.11        .266              $594.89

TOTAL PRESENT VALUE =    $48727.80

READY FOR DOUBLE-DECLINING-BALANCE METHOD? Y
```

Figure 4.12: Sample Run of Depreciation Program

```
            DOUBLE-DECLINING-BALANCE DEPRECIATION

                         INCOME         PRESENT
                         TAX            VALUE
            DEPREC-      SAVINGS        DISCOUNT          PRESENT
   YEAR     IATION       AT 35 %        FACTOR            VALUE
   ----     ------       -------        ------            -----
    1     $57500.00    $20125.00         .847           $17055.10
    2     $43125.00    $15093.80         .718           $10840.10
    3     $32343.80    $11320.30         .609            $6889.89
    4     $24257.80     $8490.23         .516            $4379.17
    5     $18193.40     $6367.68         .437            $2783.37
    6     $13645.00     $4775.76         .370            $1769.09
    7     $10233.80     $3581.82         .314            $1124.42
    8     $30701.30    $10745.50         .266            $2858.70

   TOTAL PRESENT VALUE =    $47699.80

   DO YOU WANT A SUMMARY?  Y




      SUMMARY -- AFTER TAX EFFECTS OF DEPRECIATION

      COST OF ASSET = $ 230000
      USEFUL LIFE =   8 YEARS
      TAX RATE =  35 PERCENT
      EXPECTED RATE OF RETURN ON INVESTMENT =  18 PERCENT

      PRESENT VAL UNDER STRAIGHT LINE DEPREC =    $41030.50
      PRESENT VAL UNDER SYD DEPREC =    $48727.80
      PRESENT VAL UNDER DDB DEPREC =    $47699.80
```

Figure 4.12: Sample Run of Depreciation Program (cont.)

Since we have already studied the subroutines for this program, there are really only a few other lines that require comment. They are the algorithmic centers of the three depreciation methods:

Straight Line
```
230   S1 = C / N
240   S2 = C * T1 / 100
250   S3 = S2 / N
260   S4 = S3 * A
```

Sum-of-the-Years' Digits

```
380   FOR I = 1 TO N
390       Y1 = C * S(I)
400       Y2 = Y1 * T1 / 100
410       Y3 = Y2 * D(I)
420       Y4 = Y4 + Y3
430       PRINT USING W$; I, Y1, Y2, D(I), Y3
440   NEXT I
```

Double-Declining Balance

```
530   B3 = 0
540   FOR I = 1 TO N
550       B1 = B(I) * T1 / 100
560       B2 = B1 * D(I)
570       B3 = B3 + B2
580       PRINT USING W$; I, B(I), B1, D(I), B2
590   NEXT I
```

Notice how similar these three routines are. Each of them follows the same general algorithm:

1. Calculate the yearly depreciation.
2. Calculate the total or yearly tax savings due to this depreciation.
3. Find the yearly present value of this tax savings (SYD and DDB only).
4. Find the total present value of the tax savings for the entire period.
5. Print the yearly and total values.

The SYD and DDB routines both make use of the arrays that were assigned values in the subroutines. Again, in both of these cases, the loop index I is used to increment the array elements in order to access each value exactly when it is needed. The whole process is simple yet elegant. These two routines merit careful study.

Now that we understand how arrays work, we are ready to examine some arrays of more than one dimension.

Multidimensional Arrays

Assume we are writing a program in which we often need quick access to all of the values of the present value discount factor table. We would like to avoid having to calculate each value when we need it, but we have no way of predicting in advance which row (year) or column (interest rate) of the table we will be needing.

What we need here is a two-dimensional array F(Y,R), that contains all the present value factors for a range of years and a range of interest rates. We might want to access, for example, F(10,16), which would contain the present value factor for an inflow of cash ten years from now at an expected rate of return of 16%.

It turns out that assigning values to such a two-dimensional array is almost as easy as the one-dimensional array was. The key to this problem is the use of nested loops. An inner loop can be used to increment the row numbers and an outer loop can increment the column numbers.

We will use a familiar assignment statement for this program. The only difference is that now we will be using our two-dimensional array F:

```
40   F(Y,R) = 1 / (1 + R/100)^Y
```

The inner loop increments the variable Y (on both sides of the assignment statement):

```
30   FOR Y = 1 TO 20
40       F(Y,R) = 1 / (1 + R/100)^Y
90   NEXT Y
```

The outer loop increments the variable R:

```
20   FOR R = 1 TO 20
30     FOR Y = 1 TO 20
40         F(Y,R) = 1 / (1 + R/100)^Y
90     NEXT Y
100  NEXT R
```

Of course, we need to write a **DIM** statement for the array:

```
10   DIM F(20,20)
```

We can visualize this routine's action as it fills up the array F, column by column. For every value of R, Y goes through its entire range of values, from 1 to 20. So, by the time R reaches 20, we have 20 × 20, or 400 values in the array.

We can go one step further. We can put *both* tables—the present value factors, and the annuity factors—into one array. All we need to do is add another loop (we have left room for it between lines 40 and 90), and change F to a three-dimensional array. F(Y,R,1) will hold the present value factors, and F(Y,R,2) will hold the annuity factors. Remember, we can use any variables we want to access values of the array F. Y and R are the variables we have used up to now; in this program, however, we will use a new variable, C, to sum up the columns of the present value factors. The innermost loop of our program will find the annuity factors. Before each summation we will have to initialize a new element of F(Y,E,2) to zero:

```
50    F(Y,E,2) = 0
60    FOR C = 1 TO Y
70        F(Y,E,2) = F(Y,E,2) + F(C,E,1)
80    NEXT C
```

Figure 4.13 shows the entire program, including an input/output routine that will allow us to inspect values of the two tables stored in the array F. Figure 4.14 shows a sample run.

```
10    DIM F(20,20,2)
20    FOR R = 1 TO 20
30        FOR Y = 1 TO 20
40            F(Y,R,1) = 1/(1+R/100)^Y
50            F(Y,R,2) = 0
60            FOR C = 1 TO Y
70                F(Y,R,2) = F(Y,R,2) + F(C,R,1)
80            NEXT C
90        NEXT Y
100   NEXT R
110   INPUT "YEAR, PERCENT"; Y2, P1
120   IF Y2 > 20 OR P1 > 20 GOTO 110
```

Figure 4.13: A Three-Dimensional Array for the Present Value Tables

```
130    PRINT "PRESENT VALUE OF $1 = "; F(Y2,P1,1)
140    PRINT "PRESENT VALUE OF ORDINARY ANNUITY OF $1 = "; F(Y2,P1,2)
150    PRINT: INPUT "ANOTHER VALUE"; A$
160    IF(A$ = 'Y') OR (A$ = 'YES') GOTO 110
170    END
```

Figure 4.13: Three-Dimensional Array for the Present Value Tables (cont.)

Run the program and notice how slowly it works. We can speed it up considerably by eliminating the innermost loop and calculating the annuity factors inside the second loop. The key to doing this is recognizing that each annuity factor is the sum of the *previous* annuity factor (in the same column) and the most recently computed discount factor. (Look back at Figures 4.1 and 4.2 to confirm that this is true.) Thus we can write the lines:

```
60     Y1 = Y − 1
70     F(Y,R,2) = F(Y1,R,2) + F(Y,R,1)
```

The only remaining problem is initializing the columns of the annuity factors to zero. We need a row of zeros at the top of the table.

Here finally is a good use for element zero of our array. We will initialize all the elements of row F(0,R,2) to zero. The first part of this version of the program is shown in Figure 4.15.

```
YEAR, PERCENT? 10, 15
PRESENT VALUE OF $1 =   .247185
PRESENT VALUE OF ORDINARY ANNUITY OF $1 =   5.01877

ANOTHER VALUE? Y
YEAR, PERCENT? 8, 18
PRESENT VALUE OF $1 =   .266038
PRESENT VALUE OF ORDINARY ANNUITY OF $1 =   4.07757

ANOTHER VALUE? Y
YEAR, PERCENT? 5, 20
PRESENT VALUE OF $1 =   .401878
PRESENT VALUE OF ORDINARY ANNUITY OF $1 =   2.99061

ANOTHER VALUE? N
```

Figure 4.14: Sample Run from Three-Dimensional Array Program

This program will run much faster than the first version and will produce the same results. It is worth studying both versions of this program carefully to see how multidimensional arrays are assigned values inside nested loops.

Some BASICs do not allow arrays of more than one dimension, and in any BASIC the number of dimensions and the length of each dimension is limited by the amount of memory space available.

```
10    DIM F(20,20,2)
20    FOR R = 1 TO 20
30        F(0,R,2) = 0
40        FOR Y = 1 TO 20
50            F(Y,R,1) = 1/(1 + R/100)^Y
60            Y1 = Y − 1
70            F(Y,R,2) = F(Y1,R,2) + F(Y,R,1)
80        NEXT Y
90    NEXT R
```

Figure 4.15: Using the Zeroth Element of an Array

Arrays in Other Languages

In COBOL arrays are usually referred to as *tables* and are defined in the **DATA DIVISION** with an **OCCURS** clause. For example:

```
05    PRES-VAL-TABLE OCCURS 30 TIMES          PIC 9(6).
```

defines a row of 30 six-digit values. The values would be accessed with an index in parentheses (in the **PROCEDURE DIVISION**, of course).

```
COMPUTE PRESENT-VALUE = COST * PRES-VAL-TABLE (SUBSCRIPT).
```

Do not forget that COBOL is much more particular about *spaces* than other languages we have looked at. None of the following references would work:

```
PRES-VAL-TABLE(SUBSCRIPT)
PRES-VAL-TABLE ( SUBSCRIPT)
PRES-VAL-TABLE (SUBSCRIPT )
```

In Pascal an array is typed in a **VAR** statement:

TYPE
    ARY = **ARRAY** [1 .. 30] **OF** REAL;
VAR
    PRES_VAL : ARY;

Pascal encloses subscripts in brackets rather than parentheses, which can be helpful in distinguishing function calls from arrays:

    PVAL := COST * PRES_VAL[N]

FORTRAN, as usual, is the language that most resembles BASIC in its syntax:

DIMENSION DISFAC(30)
. . .
PVAL = COST * DISFAC(N)

Summary

Arrays in BASIC are defined in a **DIM** statement, which gives the name of the array, the number of dimensions, and the length of each dimension. Access to values stored in the elements of an array is accomplished through the use of an index (integer or variable) typed in parentheses after the name of the array.

The relationship between a **FOR** loop and any arrays that it contains is an inherently powerful one. Multidimensional arrays are often used inside nested loops, as we have seen in several of the examples in this chapter.

Our main program in this chapter examines depreciation methods and the present value associated with each one. In this program we got our first glimpse of how easy it is to handle large amounts of data with arrays. In the chapters ahead we will continue to explore the use of this powerful tool.

Exercises

4.1: *Revise the program of Figure 4.11 to allow for varying tax rates over the depreciation period. Set up an array into which the user can input the expected tax rates for each year of the period. (Give the user the option of entering varying tax rates or one constant tax rate for the entire period.)*

*4.2: *Some BASICs do not have the exponentiation operation (^). How could you compute the present value without it? Rewrite the present value subroutine (Figure 4.6) for a BASIC without ^.*

*4.3: *The sum of n integers from 1 to n is equal to n(n + 1)/2. Revise the SYD subroutine (Figure 4.9) to include this algorithm.*

4.4: *How would you revise the DDB subroutine (Figure 4.10) to change to the SYD depreciation method at a certain point in the depreciation period?*

4.5: Residual value *is the remaining value of the asset at the end of the depreciation period. This value is normally deducted from the cost of the asset (at the beginning of the period, before computing the depreciation schedule) in straight-line and SYD depreciation, but not in DDB. Rewrite the input routine to accept a residual value as input, and revise the program accordingly.*

4.6: *The formula for calculating an annuity is*

$$A = \frac{1}{r}\left[1 - \frac{1}{(1 + r)^n}\right]$$

where r is the expected rate of return and n is the number of years of useful life. Rewrite the program that computes present value tables (Figure 4.13) to use this formula. Does the program run faster or slower in this form?

4.7: *Write a new output routine for the program of Figure 4.13 so that an entire row or column of either table can be requested and viewed at once.*

---

*Answer appears in Appendix A.

CHAPTER 5

Subroutines and Program Structure

IN THE FIRST FOUR CHAPTERS of this book we have examined most of the essentials of BASIC syntax. We have now reached the point where we can write programs for significant business applications. In this chapter we will touch on an issue that is important in all programming languages, whatever the application: *program structure*. Much has been written about this subject, though not typically in the context of BASIC programming.

Briefly, the goal of good organization in programming is to simplify writing, reading, debugging, and revising a program. In BASIC, one of the essential structures for meeting these goals is the subroutine. We have already studied subroutines, somewhat informally, in the COGS program of Chapter 1, and the depreciation program of Chapter 4. Now we will analyze the advantages of subroutines in more detail.

The program presented in this chapter is a simplified form of an accounting tool for general ledger transaction analysis; it records transactions on "T-accounts" and produces two reports—a trial balance and a balance sheet. In addition to subroutines, we will find two new BASIC features in this program—the **ON/GOSUB** statement, and the **READ/DATA** configuration. We will also see two illustrations of "menus" and how they are used in BASIC.

General Ledger Entries

Transaction analysis is the name sometimes given to the process of balancing ledger accounts according to the two equations of the fundamental accounting model:

Assets = Liabilities + Owners' Equity

and

Debits = Credits

These two equations are related in the way debits and credits increase or decrease assets, liabilities, and owners' equity. This function can be represented as follows:

	Assets	**Liabilities**	**Owners' Equity**
Debits	increase	decrease	decrease
Credits	decrease	increase	increase

Each entry of a transaction is balanced by at least one other entry, following the equations of the accounting model. For example, an increase in an inventory account (debit, asset) might be matched by an increase in accounts payable (credit, liability). At the end of any period, a trial balance affirms that the total debits equal the total credits, and a balance sheet details the total assets, liabilities, and owners' equity accounts.

The program that we will be studying in this chapter is an exercise illustrating the process of recording transactions. The user of this program is guided through the steps of the process in the following way:

First, prompts appear for the input of the company name and the date. Then the accounts must be initialized. In the real world, a program like this would probably take data from a *mass storage* medium (such as a tape or disk) on which accounts would be updated daily. However, our program simply asks the user to input the balance for each account from the end of the previous period.

For each account that is to be initialized, the name of the account appears along with an indication of how the account is recorded, as a debit or a credit. For example:

CASH = = = => DEBIT
?

As always, the question mark indicates that the program is ready to receive an input value.

When all the accounts have been initialized, the program checks to see whether the integrity of the accounting model has been maintained. First it checks the debit/credit equation, then the asset/liability/owners' equity formula. If either of these equations is faulty for the given input, then the user must reinitialize all the accounts. These two checks are performed every time a new transaction is recorded; an error message is always displayed when a new entry fails to maintain the balances of the accounting model.

Once a valid set of account initializations has been entered, the program offers the user several options. These options are displayed in the form of a *menu*. In computer programming, a menu is an efficient way of indicating to the user what the choices are at any given point in the execution of the program. A menu must also show the user how to indicate a chosen course of action. The menu for our transaction analysis program might be displayed many times for any given run of the program. Here is what the menu looks like:

MENU
TYPE AN INTEGER FROM 1 TO 5
1) DISPLAY AN ACCOUNT
2) ENTER A TRANSACTION
3) DISPLAY TRIAL BALANCE
4) DISPLAY BALANCE SHEET
5) QUIT
?

This menu shows how easy it is to use the features of the program. The user need only type an integer from 1 to 4 to call up one of the activities of the program, or a 5 to terminate execution. Let us examine the four major options of the program.

To see the current balance of any account, the user types a 1 when the menu is displayed. A second menu, a list of all the accounts, immediately appears. The user types in a number to indicate an account. The desired account is displayed in an abbreviated T-account form, with the debits on the left, the credits on the right, and the current balance for the account below. (See Exercise 5.6.) For example, an inventory account might look like this:

INVENTORY		
DEBIT	!	CREDIT
	!	
$5,290		$1,500
	!	
BALANCE = $3,790		DEBIT

After the account is displayed, the word:

CONTINUE?

appears. Pressing the return key at this point will cause the program to display the original menu again so that the user can choose the next activity.

Entering a 2, for a transaction entry, produces a display of the account menu again. This time the user indicates which account is to be increased or decreased by the transaction. Once an account has been chosen, the program asks a series of questions. First:

DEBIT OR CREDIT (D OR C)?

Accordingly, the user inputs a D or a C to specify which side of the account is to receive an entry. Next:

AMOUNT?

And finally:

ANOTHER ENTRY TO COMPLETE TRANSACTION (Y OR N)?

Here the user indicates whether the transaction is complete or another entry is necessary to balance the original entry. If a Y is input, the account menu is again displayed and the transaction entry process is repeated. If an N is entered, on the other hand, the program checks the balances, and, as long as the accounting equations work out properly, returns to the original option menu.

The third option simply displays the trial balance. Note that this report and the next one—the balance sheet—may be requested at any point in the program run. More transactions may be entered afterwards; the program only terminates if a 5 is entered at the main menu level.

The fourth option, the balance sheet, begins by asking:

CLOSE OUT ANY ACCOUNTS (Y OR N)?

Before preparation of the balance sheet, some accounts may be "closed out" (balanced out to zero) with their debit or credit values transferred to another account. For example, expenses and revenues are *temporary accounts* that are *closed out to* an account called Retained Earnings.

This option allows the user to perform just such an activity. If a Y is entered in response to the question above, the program asks several more questions, beginning with:

HOW MANY ACCOUNTS?

Here the user indicates the number of accounts to be closed out. When this information is entered, the program once again displays the account menu, with two questions:

WHICH ACCOUNT?

and

CLOSE TO WHICH ACCOUNT?

Both of these questions are answered with integers, specifying first the account to be closed and then the account that is to receive the balance.

When the number of accounts to be closed out has been reached, the program displays the resulting balance sheet. First the assets, then the liabilities and owners' equity accounts are displayed, showing clearly the totals for each category.

Figure 5.1 shows a sample run of this program. Study it carefully. Before we examine the program itself we will discuss the compelling reasons for using subroutines to write a program like this one.

```
COMPANY NAME? "MATTESON'S, INC."
DATE? 31 DECEMBER 1981

INITIALIZE ACCOUNTS.
INPUT BALANCE FROM END OF PREVIOUS PERIOD

CASH ====> DEBIT
? 10000
INVENTORY ====> DEBIT
? 2800
ACCOUNTS RECEIVABLE ====> DEBIT
? 3700
EQUIPMENT ====> DEBIT
? 12200
ACCOUNTS PAYABLE ====> CREDIT
? 1100
LONG-TERM DEBTS ====> CREDIT
? 6000
CAPITAL STOCK ====> CREDIT
? 10000
CONTRIBUTED CAPITAL, EOP ====> CREDIT
? 5000
RETAINED EARNINGS ====> CREDIT
? 6600
REVENUES ====> CREDIT
? 0
EXPENSES ====> DEBIT
? 0
DEBITS =     $28,700.00
CREDITS =    $28,700.00
   ASSETS         LIABILITIES              OWNERS' EQUITY
    $28,700.00         $7,100.00              $21,600.00
CONTINUE? Y


MENU
TYPE AN INTEGER FROM 1 TO 5
1) DISPLAY AN ACCOUNT
2) ENTER A TRANSACTION
3) DISPLAY TRIAL BALANCE
4) DISPLAY BALANCE SHEET
5) QUIT
? 2
```

Figure 5.1: Output from the General Ledger Program

```
WHICH ACCOUNT?
TYPE AN INTEGER FROM 1 TO   11
  1 ) CASH
  2 ) INVENTORY
  3 ) ACCOUNTS RECEIVABLE
  4 ) EQUIPMENT
  5 ) ACCOUNTS PAYABLE
  6 ) LONG-TERM DEBTS
  7 ) CAPITAL STOCK
  8 ) CONTRIBUTED CAPITAL, EOP
  9 ) RETAINED EARNINGS
 10 ) REVENUES
 11 ) EXPENSES
? 2
DEBIT OR CREDIT (D OR C)? C
AMOUNT? 800
ANOTHER ENTRY TO COMPLETE TRANSACTION (Y OR N)? Y
```

```
WHICH ACCOUNT?
TYPE AN INTEGER FROM 1 TO   11
  1 ) CASH
  2 ) INVENTORY
  3 ) ACCOUNTS RECEIVABLE
  4 ) EQUIPMENT
  5 ) ACCOUNTS PAYABLE
  6 ) LONG-TERM DEBTS
  7 ) CAPITAL STOCK
  8 ) CONTRIBUTED CAPITAL, EOP
  9 ) RETAINED EARNINGS
 10 ) REVENUES
 11 ) EXPENSES
? 11
DEBIT OR CREDIT (D OR C)? D
AMOUNT? 800
ANOTHER ENTRY TO COMPLETE TRANSACTION (Y OR N)? Y
```

```
WHICH ACCOUNT?
TYPE AN INTEGER FROM 1 TO   11
  1 ) CASH
  2 ) INVENTORY
  3 ) ACCOUNTS RECEIVABLE
  4 ) EQUIPMENT
  5 ) ACCOUNTS PAYABLE
  6 ) LONG-TERM DEBTS
  7 ) CAPITAL STOCK
  8 ) CONTRIBUTED CAPITAL, EOP
  9 ) RETAINED EARNINGS
 10 ) REVENUES
 11 ) EXPENSES
? 1
DEBIT OR CREDIT (D OR C)? D
AMOUNT? 1200
ANOTHER ENTRY TO COMPLETE TRANSACTION (Y OR N)? Y
```

Figure 5.1: Output from the General Ledger Program (cont.)

```
WHICH ACCOUNT?
TYPE AN INTEGER FROM 1 TO  11
  1 ) CASH
  2 ) INVENTORY
  3 ) ACCOUNTS RECEIVABLE
  4 ) EQUIPMENT
  5 ) ACCOUNTS PAYABLE
  6 ) LONG-TERM DEBTS
  7 ) CAPITAL STOCK
  8 ) CONTRIBUTED CAPITAL, EOP
  9 ) RETAINED EARNINGS
  10 ) REVENUES
  11 ) EXPENSES
? 10
DEBIT OR CREDIT (D OR C)? C
AMOUNT? 1200
ANOTHER ENTRY TO COMPLETE TRANSACTION (Y OR N)? N
DEBITS  =     $30,700.00
CREDITS =     $30,700.00
  ASSETS            LIABILITIES            OWNERS' EQUITY
   $29,100.00          $7,100.00             $22,000.00
CONTINUE?
```

```
MENU
TYPE AN INTEGER FROM 1 TO 5
1) DISPLAY AN ACCOUNT
2) ENTER A TRANSACTION
3) DISPLAY TRIAL BALANCE
4) DISPLAY BALANCE SHEET
5) QUIT
? 2
```

```
WHICH ACCOUNT?
TYPE AN INTEGER FROM 1 TO  11
  1 ) CASH
  2 ) INVENTORY
  3 ) ACCOUNTS RECEIVABLE
  4 ) EQUIPMENT
  5 ) ACCOUNTS PAYABLE
  6 ) LONG-TERM DEBTS
  7 ) CAPITAL STOCK
  8 ) CONTRIBUTED CAPITAL, EOP
  9 ) RETAINED EARNINGS
  10 ) REVENUES
  11 ) EXPENSES
? 3
DEBIT OR CREDIT (D OR C)? C
AMOUNT? 1750
ANOTHER ENTRY TO COMPLETE TRANSACTION (Y OR N)? Y
```

Figure 5.1: Output from the General Ledger Program (cont.)

```
WHICH ACCOUNT?
TYPE AN INTEGER FROM 1 TO   11
  1 ) CASH
  2 ) INVENTORY
  3 ) ACCOUNTS RECEIVABLE
  4 ) EQUIPMENT
  5 ) ACCOUNTS PAYABLE
  6 ) LONG-TERM DEBTS
  7 ) CAPITAL STOCK
  8 ) CONTRIBUTED CAPITAL, EOP
  9 ) RETAINED EARNINGS
 10 ) REVENUES
 11 ) EXPENSES
? 1
DEBIT OR CREDIT (D OR C)? D
AMOUNT? 1750
ANOTHER ENTRY TO COMPLETE TRANSACTION (Y OR N)? N
DEBITS =    $32,450.00
CREDITS =    $32,450.00
  ASSETS          LIABILITIES           OWNERS' EQUITY
   $29,100.00          $7,100.00          $22,000.00
CONTINUE?
```

```
MENU
TYPE AN INTEGER FROM 1 TO 5
1) DISPLAY AN ACCOUNT
2) ENTER A TRANSACTION
3) DISPLAY TRIAL BALANCE
4) DISPLAY BALANCE SHEET
5) QUIT
? 2
```

```
WHICH ACCOUNT?
TYPE AN INTEGER FROM 1 TO   11
  1 ) CASH
  2 ) INVENTORY
  3 ) ACCOUNTS RECEIVABLE
  4 ) EQUIPMENT
  5 ) ACCOUNTS PAYABLE
  6 ) LONG-TERM DEBTS
  7 ) CAPITAL STOCK
  8 ) CONTRIBUTED CAPITAL, EOP
  9 ) RETAINED EARNINGS
 10 ) REVENUES
 11 ) EXPENSES
? 4
DEBIT OR CREDIT (D OR C)? C
AMOUNT? 2440
ANOTHER ENTRY TO COMPLETE TRANSACTION (Y OR N)? Y
```

Figure 5.1: Output from the General Ledger Program (cont.)

```
WHICH ACCOUNT?
TYPE AN INTEGER FROM 1 TO  11
  1 ) CASH
  2 ) INVENTORY
  3 ) ACCOUNTS RECEIVABLE
  4 ) EQUIPMENT
  5 ) ACCOUNTS PAYABLE
  6 ) LONG-TERM DEBTS
  7 ) CAPITAL STOCK
  8 ) CONTRIBUTED CAPITAL, EOP
  9 ) RETAINED EARNINGS
  10 ) REVENUES
  11 ) EXPENSES
? 11
DEBIT OR CREDIT (D OR C)? D
AMOUNT? 2440
ANOTHER ENTRY TO COMPLETE TRANSACTION (Y OR N)? N
DEBITS =    $34,890.00
CREDITS =    $34,890.00
   ASSETS             LIABILITIES          OWNERS' EQUITY
     $26,660.00          $7,100.00            $19,560.00
CONTINUE?
```

```
MENU
TYPE AN INTEGER FROM 1 TO 5
1) DISPLAY AN ACCOUNT
2) ENTER A TRANSACTION
3) DISPLAY TRIAL BALANCE
4) DISPLAY BALANCE SHEET
5) QUIT
? 1
```

```
WHICH ACCOUNT?
TYPE AN INTEGER FROM 1 TO  11
  1 ) CASH
  2 ) INVENTORY
  3 ) ACCOUNTS RECEIVABLE
  4 ) EQUIPMENT
  5 ) ACCOUNTS PAYABLE
  6 ) LONG-TERM DEBTS
  7 ) CAPITAL STOCK
  8 ) CONTRIBUTED CAPITAL, EOP
  9 ) RETAINED EARNINGS
  10 ) REVENUES
  11 ) EXPENSES
? 10
```

Figure 5.1: Output from the General Ledger Program (cont.)

```
            REVENUES
            ----------------------------------
              DEBIT        !      CREDIT
            ----------------------------------
                           !
              $0.00        !    $1,200.00
                           !
            ----------------------------------
              BALANCE =      $1,200.00   CREDIT


    DISPLAY ANOTHER ACCOUNT? Y

    WHICH ACCOUNT?
    TYPE AN INTEGER FROM 1 TO   11
      1 ) CASH
      2 ) INVENTORY
      3 ) ACCOUNTS RECEIVABLE
      4 ) EQUIPMENT
      5 ) ACCOUNTS PAYABLE
      6 ) LONG-TERM DEBTS
      7 ) CAPITAL STOCK
      8 ) CONTRIBUTED CAPITAL, EOP
      9 ) RETAINED EARNINGS
     10 ) REVENUES
     11 ) EXPENSES
    ?11

            EXPENSES
            ----------------------------------
              DEBIT        !      CREDIT
            ----------------------------------
                           !
            $3,240.00      !      $0.00
                           !
            ----------------------------------
              BALANCE =      $3,240.00    DEBIT

    DISPLAY ANOTHER ACCOUNT? N


    MENU
    TYPE AN INTEGER FROM 1 TO 5
    1) DISPLAY AN ACCOUNT
    2) ENTER A TRANSACTION
    3) DISPLAY TRIAL BALANCE
    4) DISPLAY BALANCE SHEET
    5) QUIT
    ? 3
```

Figure 5.1: Output from the General Ledger Program (cont.)

```
                                         BALANCE
                                 --------------------------------
          ACCOUNT                DEBIT                    CREDIT
CASH                             $12,950.00                $0.00
INVENTORY                         $2,000.00                $0.00
ACCOUNTS RECEIVABLE               $1,950.00                $0.00
EQUIPMENT                         $9,760.00                $0.00
ACCOUNTS PAYABLE                      $0.00            $1,100.00
LONG-TERM DEBTS                       $0.00            $6,000.00
CAPITAL STOCK                         $0.00           $10,000.00
CONTRIBUTED CAPITAL, EOP              $0.00            $5,000.00
RETAINED EARNINGS                     $0.00            $6,600.00
REVENUES                              $0.00            $1,200.00
EXPENSES                          $3,240.00                $0.00
**** TOTALS ****                 $29,900.00           $29,900.00
CONTINUE?


MENU
TYPE AN INTEGER FROM 1 TO 5
1) DISPLAY AN ACCOUNT
2) ENTER A TRANSACTION
3) DISPLAY TRIAL BALANCE
4) DISPLAY BALANCE SHEET
5) QUIT
? 4

CLOSE OUT ANY ACCOUNTS (Y OR N)? Y
HOW MANY ACCOUNTS? 2


WHICH ACCOUNT?
TYPE AN INTEGER FROM 1 TO   11
  1 ) CASH
  2 ) INVENTORY
  3 ) ACCOUNTS RECEIVABLE
  4 ) EQUIPMENT
  5 ) ACCOUNTS PAYABLE
  6 ) LONG-TERM DEBTS
  7 ) CAPITAL STOCK
  8 ) CONTRIBUTED CAPITAL, EOP
  9 ) RETAINED EARNINGS
  10 ) REVENUES
  11 ) EXPENSES
? 10
CLOSE TO WHICH ACCOUNT? 9
```

Figure 5.1: Output from the General Ledger Program (cont.)

```
WHICH ACCOUNT?
TYPE AN INTEGER FROM 1 TO 11
  1 ) CASH
  2 ) INVENTORY
  3 ) ACCOUNTS RECEIVABLE
  4 ) EQUIPMENT
  5 ) ACCOUNTS PAYABLE
  6 ) LONG-TERM DEBTS
  7 ) CAPITAL STOCK
  8 ) CONTRIBUTED CAPITAL, EOP
  9 ) RETAINED EARNINGS
 10 ) REVENUES
 11 ) EXPENSES
? 11
CLOSE TO WHICH ACCOUNT? 9
```

```
                    MATTESON'S, INC.
                    BALANCE SHEET
                    31 DECEMBER 1981
        ASSETS
CASH                        $12,950.00
INVENTORY                    $2,000.00
ACCOUNTS RECEIVABLE          $1,950.00
EQUIPMENT                    $9,760.00
**** TOTAL ASSETS                        $26,660.00
CONTINUE?


        LIABILITIES
ACCOUNTS PAYABLE             $1,100.00
LONG-TERM DEBTS             $6,000.00
**** TOTAL LIABILITIES                    $7,100.00

        OWNERS' EQUITY
CAPITAL STOCK              $10,000.00
CONTRIBUTED CAPITAL, EOP    $5,000.00
RETAINED EARNINGS           $4,560.00
**** TOTAL OWNERS' EQUITY                $19,560.00
**** TOTAL LIABILITIES PLUS
        OWNERS' EQUITY                   $26,660.00
CONTINUE?
```

```
MENU
TYPE AN INTEGER FROM 1 TO 5
1) DISPLAY AN ACCOUNT
2) ENTER A TRANSACTION
3) DISPLAY TRIAL BALANCE
4) DISPLAY BALANCE SHEET
5) QUIT
? 5
```

Figure 5.1: Output from the General Ledger Program (cont.)

Subroutine Syntax in BASIC

As we have seen already, the general form of the subroutine call in BASIC is this:

GOSUB A

where A is a line number used in the program. Line A, which may be located either before or after the line that contains the **GOSUB** statement, is the first line of the subroutine. The end of the subroutine is marked by the word **RETURN**, which sends control of the program back to the line following the **GOSUB** statement.

Another form of the **GOSUB** statement is **ON/GOSUB**:

ON N **GOSUB** A, B, C, D, . . .

where N is a variable and A, B, C, D, etc., are line numbers. We will find an example of this statement in the general ledger program:

190   **ON** M9 **GOSUB** 1500, 3000, 5500, 6000, 9999

This statement sends control of the program to one of five lines, depending on the value of M9:

if M9 equals	then GOSUB
1	1500
2	3000
3	5500
4	6000
5	9999

Notice that the correct range of M9 (1 to 5) is defined by the number of lines listed after the word **GOSUB**. The **ON** statement can also be combined with **GOTO**, in the following form:

ON N **GOTO** A, B, C, D, . . .

Unfortunately, the **ON** statement must be used with caution. Its action is predictable only if its variable falls within the prescribed range of values. In our example, if M9 has a value from 1 to 5, then one of five subroutines will be called. But what happens if M9 equals 6? The answer depends on the version of BASIC we are using. One of three events might occur:

1. The program might simply ignore the **GOSUB** and proceed to the statement following the **ON** statement.

2. Control of the program might pass to the last line number indicated in the **ON/GOSUB** statement (in our example, 9999).

3. Execution of the program might end abnormally, with an error message.

We can eliminate this uncertainty by testing the value of the variable before execution of an **ON** statement. For example:

```
170   INPUT M9
180   IF M9 < 1 OR M9 > 5 GOTO 170
190   ON M9 GOSUB 1500, 3000, 5500, 6000, 9999
```

In this sequence, if M9 is outside of the correct range, then control branches back to the **INPUT** statement for a new value. With this problem solved, the **ON/GOSUB** statement can be a powerful way to implement a range of choices in a program. We will use **ON/GOSUB** for the main menu of our general ledger program.

A discussion of the use of subroutines leads us to a much larger issue—program structure. The subroutine is a tool that permits a *top-down, modular* approach to writing programs. We will begin to understand what is meant by these terms as we outline the advantages of subroutines in the next section.

Program Structure

The most obvious reason for using a subroutine in BASIC is simply to avoid extra typing when a block of instructions is needed more than once in a program. We saw an example of this situation in the depreciation program of Chapter 4. In that program, the subroutine at line 1000 prints a somewhat complicated set of headings for the depreciation tables. Since the same headings were used twice—both for the sum-of-the-years'-digits and the double-declining-balance depreciation methods—we isolated the heading instructions in the form of a subroutine. Then, whenever we required that set of headings for a table we only needed to type:

GOSUB 1000

As we begin writing long programs that perform many tasks, we find that subroutines not only help us avoid extra typing, but also help us organize the very process of writing a program. The key to this process is to isolate each different task of the program, almost as if the algorithm of each task were a program in itself. This approach is often used when programmers work together as a team on a very large program; it also turns out to be the best approach in most cases when a single programmer is writing an entire program.

When we have determined the main tasks that are to be performed by a program, we begin by writing the *main program* section. In BASIC this section is normally located at the very beginning of the program. It is typically short, and its main function is simply to call the subroutines that perform the various tasks of the program. This kind of organization is often referred to as the top-down approach.

The general ledger program was developed using this approach. The main program calls six subroutines in all. Some of these subroutines call subroutines of their own in turn. The "structure chart" of Figure 5.2 illustrates the relationship between the main program and the subroutines below it.

One important feature of top-down program development is that it allows subroutines to be tested as they are written. At the time that we write the main program, we can also write temporary "stubs" in the place of each subroutine; for example:

```
5000   PRINT "ASSETS = LIABILITIES + OWNERS' EQUITY."
5010   PRINT "CHECK NOT IMPLEMENTED YET."
5020   RETURN
```

Let us say we have written the first two subroutines called by the main program—the string initialization subroutine and the account initialization subroutine. In addition, the subroutine that checks the debits and credits in the initial account balances is complete. However, the subroutine that checks for the other equation of the accounting model—assets equals liabilities plus owners' equity—has not been written yet. We would like to test the subroutines that are complete, even though one of these completed subroutines contains a call to a subroutine that does not exist yet.

This is where the stub comes in. When the account initialization subroutine calls the asset/liability/owners' equity check subroutine, the stub that is temporarily representing the latter routine simply prints out the following message:

ASSETS = LIABILITIES + OWNERS' EQUITY.

CHECK NOT IMPLEMENTED YET.

and then returns control of the program back to the account initialization subroutine. The test run of the program is not interrupted, as it would be if a **GOSUB** statement called a subroutine that did not exist.

In this way, the top-down modular approach allows step-by-step writing and testing of each subroutine until the program is complete. We should note that the terms "top-down" and "modular" have different levels of meaning, depending on who is using them. Their use in this discussion is somewhat informal; however, as we study the subroutines of the transaction analysis program, the wisdom of this general approach to programming will become clear.

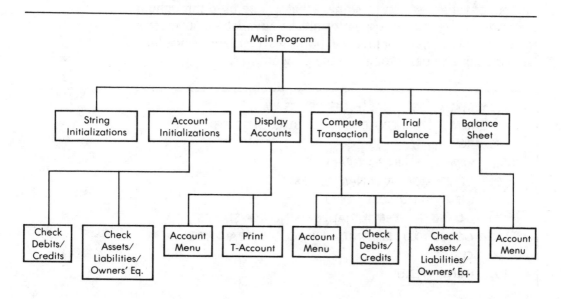

Figure 5.2: Structure Chart of Transaction Analysis Program

The Program, Step by Step

Figure 5.3 shows the main program section of the transaction analysis program. The subroutine calls are at lines 70, 80, and 190. The main program also has input statements (lines 50 and 60) for the company name and the date. These two pieces of information are necessary for the balance sheet.

Lines 100 to 160 display the menu, line 170 accepts the input response to the menu, and line 180 validates the input before the **ON/GOSUB** statement is executed. Finally, the **GOTO** statement of line 210 branches back to the beginning of the menu to form a loop. Execution of this loop continues until the user types a 5 to terminate the program; the **ON** statement then branches to:

    9999   **END**

With its subroutine calls and its continuing loop, this main program section clearly controls all the action of this detailed program, yet these lines were easy to plan and write, and their purpose is immediately evident to anyone reading the program.

The first subroutine of the program, listed in Figure 5.4, sets a number of variables—mostly strings—that will be used throughout the program. We ordinarily speak of initializing *variables,* but most of these variables are, for all practical purposes, *constants,* since they keep the same values throughout the program.

```
10   REM       GENERAL LEDGER PROGRAM
20   REM       D. HERGERT          31 AUGUST 1981
30   REM
40   REM       MAIN PROGRAM
50   INPUT "COMPANY NAME"; N5$
60   INPUT "DATE"; D5$
70   GOSUB 500 : REM INITIALIZE STRING CONSTANTS
80   GOSUB 1000 : REM INITIALIZE ACCOUNT BALANCES
90   CLS
100  PRINT "MENU"
```

Figure 5.3: Main Program

```
110   PRINT "TYPE AN INTEGER FROM 1 TO 5"
120   PRINT "1) DISPLAY AN ACCOUNT"
130   PRINT "2) ENTER A TRANSACTION"
140   PRINT "3) DISPLAY TRIAL BALANCE"
150   PRINT "4) DISPLAY BALANCE SHEET"
160   PRINT "5) QUIT"
170   INPUT M9
180   IF M9 < 1 OR M9 > 5 GOTO 170
190   ON M9 GOSUB 1500, 3000, 5500, 6000, 9999
200   CLS
210   GOTO 100
```

Figure 5.3: Main Program (cont.)

This subroutine uses the **READ/DATA** syntax to assign values to the variables involved. **READ/DATA** is actually a way of inputting data values into a program. However, instead of entering data from the keyboard during the execution of the program, the programmer includes the data in the program itself. The **DATA** statement creates a kind of "file" of information that is reliably available each time the program is run. As we will see in this example, **READ/DATA** can sometimes be a more convenient way to supply data to a program than through the interactive **INPUT** statement.

The syntax of the **READ/DATA** sequence is as follows:

> **READ** A, B, C, . . .
> **DATA** V1, V2, V3 . . .

where A, B, C, etc., are variables, and V1, V2, V3, etc., are *literal* values (i.e., integers, real numbers, or strings). The **READ** statement instructs BASIC to assign values to the variables A, B, C, etc., from a **DATA** statement. Data is read consecutively from all the **DATA** statements in the program. The programmer must therefore make sure that the sequence of variables in the **READ** statements corresponds correctly to the sequence of values in the **DATA** statements. (The **DATA** statements are usually grouped together at the end of a program or subroutine, but this is not required.) If a **READ** statement is encountered at a point where there is no data left to be read, then the program ends with an error message. (The **RESTORE** statement, which is not used in the general ledger program, instructs BASIC to start reading data over again from the very first **DATA** statement.)

The first **READ** statement in this subroutine, at line 630, assigns values to the variables N, A, L, and O from the first **DATA** statement, at line 770:

```
630   READ N, A, L, O

      . . .

770   DATA 11, 4, 2, 5
```

```
500   REM        STRING CONSTANTS SUBROUTINE
510   REM
520   REM        VARIABLE NAMES
530   REM        N$                  ARRAY OF ACCOUNT NAMES
540   REM        M$                  DUPLICATE OF ACCOUNT NAMES
550   REM        F1$ — F4$           FORMAT STRINGS
560   REM        T, F                BOOLEAN CONSTANTS TRUE AND FALSE
570   REM        T5$                 ARRAY OF DEBIT OR CREDIT INDICATORS
580   REM        N                   NUMBER OF ACCOUNTS
590   REM        A                   NUMBER OF ASSET ACCOUNTS
600   REM        L                   NUMBER OF LIABILITY ACCOUNTS
610   REM        O                   NUMBER OF OWNERS' EQUITY ACCOUNTS
620   REM
630   READ N, A, L, O
640   DIM N$(N), M$(N), T5$(N)
650   FOR I = 1 TO N
660       READ N$(I), T5$(I)
670   NEXT I
680   T1$ = "DEBIT"
690   T2$ = "CREDIT"
700   F1$ = "$$##,#####.##"
710   F2$ = "$$##,#####.##    $$##,#####.##    $$##,#####.##"
720   F3$ = "  $$##,#####.##    $$##,#####.##"
730   F4$ = "   BALANCE = $$##,#####.##"
```

Figure 5.4: Subroutine to Initialize String Constants

```
740   F5$ = "_ _ _ _ _ _ _ _ _ _ _ _ _ _ _ _ _ _ _ _ _ _ _ _ _ _ _ _ _ _"
750   F = 0
760   T = NOT F
770   DATA 11, 4, 2, 5
780   DATA "CASH", "D", "INVENTORY", "D", "ACCOUNTS RECEIVABLE"
790   DATA "D", "EQUIPMENT", "D", "ACCOUNTS PAYABLE", "C"
800   DATA "LONG—TERM DEBTS", "C", "CAPITAL STOCK", "C",
810   DATA "CONTRIBUTED CAP, EOP", "C", "RETAINED EARNINGS", "C"
820   DATA "REVENUES", "C", "EXPENSES", "D"
830   RETURN
```

Figure 5.4: Subroutine to Initialize String Constants (cont.)

The values in line 770 represent the total number of accounts, and the number of asset, liability, and owners' equity accounts, respectively.

A **DIM** statement follows this first **READ** statement:

```
640   DIM N$(N), M$(N), T5$(N)
```

This line illustrates an extremely valuable feature that we have not yet discussed. Unfortunately, it is a variation that not all BASICs allow. Recall that all the **DIM** statements that we have seen up to now have defined the length of arrays with literals rather than variables. For example:

```
DIM B(30)
```

Often, however, we do not know in advance how large an array we will need in a program, and it is thus more convenient to set the length of the array from an input value. This is the case in the general ledger program. A user of this program might well wish to change the number of accounts that the program handles. *Every feature of this program has been written to make such a change as easy as possible.* One of the keys to this easy revisability is the **DIM** statement that allows variable array lengths.

Here is how this feature works in our program. The variable N is assigned a value—11, as the program stands now—via the **READ/DATA** statements. Then the three arrays N$, M$, and T5$ are each dimensioned to the length specified by the value of N. Since the **DATA** statements now contain eleven accounts, it would be inefficient to allocate more than eleven elements for the arrays that will store information on those accounts. Specifying a fixed array length, on the other hand, would make changes in this length difficult. Clearly the best technique to use here is to read the length of the arrays as input—either via an **INPUT** statement or a **READ/DATA** sequence.

Next, a **FOR** loop is used to assign values to the elements of the arrays N$ and T5$. Again the value of N is essential, since it is used to define the range of the **FOR** loop:

```
650   FOR I = 1 TO N
660      READ N$(I), T5$(I)
670   NEXT I
```

The array N$ holds the names of the accounts, and the corresponding elements of the array T5$ indicate whether an account will be initialized as a debit or a credit. Notice that in the **DATA** statements, lines 780 to 820, each account name is followed by a "D" or a "C"; these single-letter indicators are entered into array T5$. (Array M$, which is also dimensioned in the **DIM** statement, is not used until the balance sheet subroutine; we will discuss its role when we reach that routine.)

Following the **FOR** loop, several more string "constants" are set, including four format strings (F1 to F4) for use in **PRINT USING** statements.

Finally, at the end of this subroutine we see the following two statements:

```
750   F = 0
760   T = NOT F
```

Recall from Chapter 2 that BASIC evaluates a false statement as 0 and a true statement as either 1 or −1. Some programming languages—Pascal, for example—have the Boolean constants TRUE and FALSE built into the language. BASIC does not, but in this program we will see a technique for creating these constants.

To summarize, the most important feature of this first subroutine is that it allows the user to revise the program in an essential way by revising only the **DATA** statements. Any number or combination of ledger accounts can be handled by this program. We follow three simple steps to change the accounts:

1. In the **DATA** statement of line 770, we write four integers: the total number of accounts, the number of asset accounts, the number of liability accounts, and the number of owners' equity accounts.

2. In the **DATA** statements that follow, we write the names of the accounts in this order: assets, liabilities, owners' equity. (Account names must be separated by commas, but do not need to be in quotes unless a name itself contains a comma.)

3. Following each account name, we write a D or a C, indicating how the account is initialized—as a debit or a credit.

As we will see, the variables N, A, L, and O and the arrays N$ and T5$ are used throughout this program to handle and display account information. Since all of these variables are assigned values stored in the **DATA** statements, this program provides a simple method for revising the data—and the output—of the program.

Next we will look at the account initialization subroutine, which is shown in Figure 5.5. This subroutine accepts input from the keyboard for the beginning balances of all the accounts. These balances are stored in the array A1, defined in the **DIM** statement of line 1105:

        1105   **DIM** A1(N,2), A5(N,2)

(Array A5 is used in the balance sheet subroutine.) A1 is a two-dimensional array. The first dimension is N elements long, to hold all of the accounts; the second dimension is two elements long, to hold the debits and the credits for each account. Thus, for an account N, the debits are stored in A1(N,1) and the credits are stored in A1(N,2).

```
1000    REM     ACCOUNT INITIALIZATION SUBROUTINE
1010    REM
1020    REM     VARIABLE NAMES
1030    REM     A1          ARRAY OF ACCOUNTS WITH DEBITS AND CREDITS
1035    REM     A5          DUPLICATE ARRAY OF ACCOUNTS
1040    REM     C3          SWITCH (T OR F) FOR BALANCE CHECK
1050    REM
```

Figure 5.5: Account Initialization Subroutine

```
1060    PRINT
1070    PRINT "INITIALIZE ACCOUNTS."
1080    PRINT "INPUT BALANCE FROM END OF PREVIOUS PERIOD."
1090    PRINT
1100    Z$ = "====>"
1105    DIM A1(N,2), A5(N,2)
1110    REM      INPUT LOOP
1120    FOR I = 1 TO N
1130      PRINT N$(I); Z$;
1140      IF T5$(I) = "C" GOTO 1180
1150      PRINT T1$
1160      INPUT A1(I,1)
1170      GOTO 1200
1180      PRINT T2$
1190      INPUT A1(I,2)
1200    NEXT I
1210    REM      CHECK BALANCES
1220    REM      IF INCORRECT, REINITIALIZE.
1230    REM
1235    M9 = 0  : REM SET FOR CORRECT ERROR MESSAGE
1240    REM      1) DEBITS = CREDITS
1250    REM
1260    C3 = F : REM     INITIALIZE SWITCH TO FALSE
1270    GOSUB 4500
1280    IF C3 THEN 1120
1290    REM      2) ASSETS = LIABILITIES + OWNERS' EQUITY
1300    REM
1310    C3 = F : REM     INITIALIZE SWITCH TO FALSE
1320    GOSUB 5000
1330    IF C3 THEN 1120
1340    RETURN
```

Figure 5.5: Account Initialization Subroutine (cont.)

The **FOR** loop in lines 1120 to 1200 provides the appropriate prompts, and accepts the input to initialize all N accounts. Recall that the array T5$ contains a "D" or a "C" for each account, and the strings T1$ and T2$ hold "DEBITS" and "CREDITS", respectively. Thus, for each account I, either lines 1150 to 1160 or lines 1180 to 1190 are executed, depending on the value of T5$(I). The input statement at line 1160 stores debits in A1(I,1); the input statement at line 1190 stores credits in A1(I,2).

After the balances are input, the account initialization subroutine calls the two "check" subroutines to see if the integrity of the accounting equations has been maintained. The subroutine calls are at lines 1270 and 1320. Here is the reason for the Boolean constants T and F that we created previously. Notice in each case that a variable C3 is initialized to the value of F before each subroutine call and then tested in an **IF** statement after the call; for example:

```
1260   C3 = F
1270   GOSUB 4500
1280   IF C3 THEN 1120
```

We will see that both of the "check" subroutines switch the value of C3 to the value of T if the accounting equations do not balance. The accounts must then be reinitialized before the program can continue; thus, control is branched back to line 1120—the beginning of the input loop—to start the process over again.

The "check" subroutines are displayed in Figures 5.6 and 5.7. Both of these routines follow the same format. They begin by adding up the accounts—either all the debits and credits (lines 4550 to 4580), or all the assets, liabilities, and owners' equities (lines 5040 to 5170). They then display the totals. In each case, if the equations balance out correctly then they return control to the calling subroutine:

```
4630   IF T1 = T2 THEN RETURN
```

```
5210   IF A2 = L2 + O2 THEN RETURN
```

Otherwise, an error message is displayed, and the variable C3 is switched to "true" to indicate that the equations do not balance.

```
4500   REM       DEBITS/CREDITS CHECK SUBROUTINE
4510   REM
4520   REM       FIND TOTAL DEBITS AND CREDITS
4530   T1 = 0
4540   T2 = 0
4550   FOR I = 1 TO N
4560       T1 = T1 + A1(I,1)
4570       T2 = T2 + A1(I,2)
4580   NEXT I
4590   PRINT "DEBITS = ";
4600   PRINT USING F1$; T1
4610   PRINT "CREDITS = ";
4620   PRINT USING F1$; T2
4630   IF (T1 = T2) THEN RETURN
4640   PRINT "* * * * * * * * * * * * * * * * * * * * * * * * *"
4650   PRINT "DEBITS NOT EQUAL TO CREDITS"
4660   IF M9 = 2 THEN PRINT " . . . CONTINUE TRANSACTION"
4670   IF M9 = 0 THEN PRINT " . . . REINITIALIZE ACCOUNTS"
4680   INPUT "CONTINUE"; Z9$
4690   C3 = T : REM SET SWITCH TO TRUE
4700   RETURN
```

Figure 5.6: Debits/Credits Check Subroutine

```
5000   REM       ASSETS/LIABILITIES/OWNERS'EQUITY
5010   REM       CHECK SUBROUTINE
5020   REM
5030   REM       TOTAL ASSETS = A2
5040   A2 = 0
5050   FOR I = 1 TO A
5060       A2 = A2 + (A1(I,1) − A1(I,2))
5070   NEXT I
5080   REM       TOTAL LIABILITIES = L2
5090   L2 = 0
```

Figure 5.7: Assets/Liabilities/Owners' Equity Check Subroutine

```
5100    FOR I = 1+A TO A+L
5110        L2 = L2 + (A1(I,2) − A1(I,1))
5120    NEXT I
5130    REM        TOTAL OWNERS' EQUITY = O2
5140    O2 = 0
5150    FOR I = 1+A+L TO N
5160        O2 = O2 + (A1(I,2) − A1(I,1))
5170    NEXT I
5180    PRINT " ASSETS      LIABILITIES      OWNERS' EQUITY"
5190    PRINT USING F2$; A2, L2, O2
5200    INPUT "CONTINUE"; Z9$
5210    IF A2 = L2 + O2 THEN RETURN
5220    PRINT "******************************"
5230    PRINT "ASSETS NOT EQUAL TO LIABILITIES"
5240    PRINT "PLUS OWNERS' EQUITY."
5250    IF M9 = 0 THEN PRINT " . . . CONTINUE TRANSACTION"
5260    IF M9 = 2 THEN PRINT " . . . REINITIALIZE ACCOUNTS."
5270    INPUT "CONTINUE"; Z9$
5280    C3 = T : REM SET SWITCH TO TRUE
5290    RETURN
```

Figure 5.7: Assets/Liabilities/Owners' Equity Check Subroutine (cont.)

These two subroutines illustrate another technique that we will see elsewhere in this program. Examine lines 4680, 5200, and 5270; they are all the same:

INPUT "CONTINUE"; Z9$

The **INPUT** instruction delays the program until the prompt is answered, allowing the user to examine a "screenful" of information before the screen is cleared and another subroutine is called. To continue the program, the user may simply press the return key when the prompt:

CONTINUE?

is displayed.

The account display subroutine shows the current state of any of the accounts. It begins by displaying a list (in menu form) of all the accounts, and prompting the user to choose the account that is to be displayed. It then draws the T-account on the screen: debits on the left, credits on the right, and the balance (debit or credit) below. To perform these tasks, the account display subroutine calls two other routines—the account menu and the print T-account subroutines.

The "main" subroutine, starting at line 1500, is shown in Figure 5.8. Notice that this subroutine has only four executable statements, two of which are subroutine calls. The subroutine at line 7500 (Figure 5.9) displays the account menu, and the subroutine at line 2500 (Figure 5.10) displays the T-account.

```
1500   REM        ACCOUNT DISPLAY SUBROUTINE
1510   REM
1520   GOSUB 7500 : REM ACCOUNT MENU
1530   REM        MENU SUBROUTINE "RETURNS" INDEX INTO
1540   REM        ARRAYS IN THE VARIABLE M3
1550   GOSUB 2500 : REM PRINT T—ACCOUNT
1560   INPUT "DISPLAY ANOTHER ACCOUNT"; A7$
1570   IF A7$ = "Y" OR A7$ = "YES" GOTO 1520
1580   RETURN
```

Figure 5.8: Account Display Subroutine

```
7500   REM        ACCOUNT MENU SUBROUTINE
7510   REM
7520   CLS : PRINT
7530   PRINT "WHICH ACCOUNT?"
7540   PRINT "TYPE AN INTEGER FROM 1 TO "; N
7550   FOR I = 1 TO N
7560      PRINT I; ") "; N$(I)
7570   NEXT I
7580   INPUT M3
7590   IF (M3 < 1) OR (M3 > N) GOTO 7580
7600   RETURN
```

Figure 5.9: Account Menu Subroutine

The account menu subroutine uses a **FOR** loop to display a numbered list of all the account names held in the array N$:

```
7550    FOR I = 1 TO N
7560       PRINT I; ") "; N$(I)
7570    NEXT I
```

It then prompts for an input value, which it stores in M3. If this value is not between 1 and N, then it branches back to the **INPUT** statement for a valid input value:

```
7590    IF (M3 < 1) OR (M3 > N) GOTO 7580
```

The print T-account subroutine uses the value of M3 as an index into the arrays N$ and A1. First it prints the name of the account:

```
2520    PRINT TAB(8); N$(M3)
```

Then it displays the current debits and credits of the account:

```
2580    PRINT USING F3$; A1(M3,1), A1(M3,2)
```

```
2500    REM        PRINT T — ACCOUNT SUBROUTINE
2510    REM
2520    PRINT TAB(8); N$(M3)
2530    PRINT TAB(8); F5$
2540    PRINT TAB(11); T1$; TAB(24); "!"; TAB(31); T2$
2550    PRINT TAB(8); F5$
2560    PRINT TAB(24); "!"
2570    PRINT TAB(2);
2580    PRINT USING F3$; A1(M3,1), A1(M3,2) : REM DEBITS,CREDITS
2590    PRINT TAB(24); "!"
2600    PRINT TAB(8); F5$
2610    PRINT TAB(6);
2620    PRINT USING F4$; ABS(A1(M3,1) — A1(M3,2)); : REM BALANCE
2630    PRINT " ";
2640    IF A1(M3,1) > A1(M3,2) THEN PRINT T1$
2650    IF A1(M3,2) > A1(M3,1) THEN PRINT T2$
2660    PRINT
2670    RETURN
```

Figure 5.10: Print T-Account Subroutine

And finally, the subroutine calculates and prints the balance of the account. Notice the use of the absolute value function, **ABS**; this function simply returns the positive value of its argument:

2620   **PRINT USING** F4$; **ABS**(A1(M3,1)−A1(M3,2));

It also indicates, via the two **IF** statements at lines 2640 and 2650, whether the balance is a debit or a credit.

The transaction subroutine is shown in Figure 5.11. This subroutine allows the user to record a transaction, i.e., to increase the debits or credits of any combination of accounts. However, any combination of changes must maintain the balance of the accounts; the user may not return to the main menu level (the main program) until both of the accounting model equations are verified.

```
3000   REM        TRANSACTION SUBROUTINE
3010   REM
3020   GOSUB 7500 : REM ACCOUNT MENU
3030   INPUT "DEBIT OR CREDIT (D OR C)"; A7$
3040   IF A7$ <> "D" AND A7$ <> "C" GOTO 3030
3050   INPUT "AMOUNT"; T3
3060   IF A7$ = "D" THEN A1(M3,1) = A1(M3,1) + T3
3070   IF A7$ = "C" THEN A1(M3,2) = A1(M3,2) + T3
3080   INPUT "ANOTHER ENTRY TO COMPLETE TRANSACTION (Y OR N)"; A7$
3090   IF A7$ <> "Y" AND A7$ <> "N" GOTO 3080
3100   IF A7$ = "Y" GOTO 3020
3110   REM        CHECK BALANCES
3120   REM        1) DEBITS = CREDITS
3130   C3 = F : REM        INITIALIZE SWITCH TO FALSE
3140   GOSUB 4500
3150   IF C3 THEN 3020
3160   REM        2) ASSETS = LIABILITIES + OWNERS' EQUITY
3170   C3 = F : REM        INITIALIZE SWITCH TO FALSE
3180   GOSUB 5000
3190   IF C3 THEN 3020
3200   RETURN
```

Figure 5.11: Transaction Subroutine

The transaction subroutine begins by calling the account menu subroutine (at line 7500) to give the user a choice of accounts. Once an account has been chosen, two **INPUT** lines prompt for information about the transaction. First the user must indicate whether the increase is to go on the debit or credit side of the account (line 3030); this information is stored in the variable A7$. Then the amount of the change is entered into the variable T3. One of two **IF** statements (lines 3060 and 3070) is used to increase the correct element of A1 by the amount T3. Depending on the value of A7$, either the debits (A1(M3,1)) or the credits (A1(M3,2)) are increased.

The user may change as many accounts as necessary. Line 3100 branches control back to the beginning of the subroutine as long as the user wishes to continue making entries. Finally, when the entries are complete, the two "check" subroutines are called (at lines 4500 and 5000) to confirm that the accounts balance out. Again the variable C3 is used as a "switch"—with the values T or F—to indicate the results of the "check" subroutines. If C3 becomes true, then control is passed to the beginning of the transaction subroutine for additional entries.

The trial balance subroutine, shown in Figure 5.12, uses a **FOR** loop (lines 5570 to 5660) to balance and display each account and to find the total debits and credits (stored in T1 and T2, respectively). The trial balance sheet is completed with a total line to confirm that debits equal credits. This subroutine does not need to check the balance before displaying the balance sheet, because a check is made after each account transaction.

The balance sheet subroutine (Figure 5.13) is also primarily devoted to printing out a report. This subroutine, however, must offer the user the opportunity to close out any accounts, which means making changes in the current account information. Since we may not want to lose current data on the accounts that are to be closed out, the balance sheet subroutine begins by making copies of the account name array (N$) and the account value array (A1). The **FOR** loop in lines 6060 to 6090 is used to duplicate both arrays at once.

Thus, in this subroutine A5 and M$ are used in place of A1 and N$ to represent the account information. If there are accounts to close out, the user is asked how many, and the **FOR** loop at line 6140 repeats once for each close-out. The account menu subroutine is called to find out which account is to be closed. Then the user must indicate which account is to receive the balance of the closing. The numbers of these two accounts are assigned to M3 and M4, respectively. The value input for M4 is validated as follows:

6165   **IF** M$(M4) = "CLOSED" **OR** M3 = M4

OR M4 < 1 **OR** M4 > N **GOTO** 6160

This line tests for three conditions: the account represented by M4 must be one that is still open, must not be the account that is currently being closed, and must be within the actual range of account numbers.

Finally, the name of account M3 is replaced by "CLOSED" (line 6170), and the debits and credits of the account are added to account M4 (lines 6180 and 6190).

```
5500   REM        TRIAL BALANCE SUBROUTINE
5510   REM
5520   PRINT TAB(40); "BALANCE"
5530   PRINT TAB(31); F5$
5540   PRINT " ACCOUNT"; TAB(31); T1$; TAB(54); T2$
5550   T1 = 0
5560   T2 = 0
5570   FOR I TO N
5580      IF A1(I,2) > A1(I,1) GOTO 5630
5590      PRINT N$(I); TAB(26);
5600      PRINT USING F3$; A1(I,1) — A1(I,2), 0
5610      T1 = A1(I,1) — A1(I,2) + T1
5620      GOTO 5660
5630      PRINT N$(I); TAB(26);
5640      PRINT USING F3$; 0, A1(I,2) — A1(I,1)
5650      T2 = A1(I,2) — A1(I,1) + T2
5660   NEXT I
5665   PRINT "**** TOTALS ****"; TAB(26);
5670   PRINT USING F3$; T1,T2
5680   INPUT "CONTINUE"; Z9$
5690   RETURN
```

Figure 5.12: Trial Balance Subroutine

The balances for assets, liabilities, and owners' equity accounts are each printed out in an individual **FOR** loop. Before an account is printed, however, its name is checked in the array M$; if the name has been replaced by "CLOSED" then a **GOTO** statement jumps to the end of the loop:

6270   **IF** M$(I) = "CLOSED" **GOTO** 6310

These lines (6270, 6350, and 6450) ensure that closed accounts are not included on the balance sheet.

The final lines of the balance sheet subroutine display the totals for assets, liabilities, and owners' equity, confirming that the accounts are balanced. Note that the user may still continue transactions after a balance sheet has been displayed. The original data on all the accounts are still secure in the arrays N$ and A1.

```
6000   REM      BALANCE SHEET SUBROUTINE
6010   REM
6020   REM      MAKE COPIES OF A1 IN A5,
6030   REM      AND N$ IN M$; USE A5 AND M$
6040   REM      FOR THIS SUBROUTINE.
6050   REM
6060   FOR I = 1 TO N
6070      A5(I,1) = A1(I,1)
6080      A5(I,2) = A1(I,2)
6085      M$(I) = N$(I)
6090   NEXT I
6100   INPUT "CLOSE OUT ANY ACCOUNTS (Y OR N)"; A5$
6110   IF A5$ <> "Y" AND A5$ <> "N" GOTO 6100
6120   IF A5$ = "N" GOTO 6205
6130   INPUT "HOW MANY ACCOUNTS"; C1
6140   FOR J = 1 TO C1
6150      GOSUB 7500 : REM MENU
6160      INPUT "CLOSE TO WHICH ACCOUNT"; M4
6165      IF M$(M4) = "CLOSED" OR M3 = M4 OR M4 < 1 OR M4 > N GOTO 6160
```

Figure 5.13: The Balance Sheet Subroutine

```
6170    M$(M3) = "CLOSED"
6180      A5(M4,1) = A5(M4,1) + A1(M3,1)
6190      A5(M4,2) = A5(M4,2) + A1(M3,2)
6200    NEXT J
6205    CLS
6210    REM        BEGIN BALANCE SHEET
6220    PRINT TAB(16); N5$ : REM NAME OF COMPANY
6230    PRINT TAB(16); "BALANCE SHEET"
6240    PRINT TAB(16); D5$ : REM DATE
6250    PRINT "    ASSETS"
6255    A2 = 0
6260    FOR I = 1 TO A
6270      IF M$(I) = "CLOSED" GOTO 6310
6280      PRINT M$(I); TAB(26);
6290      PRINT USING F1$; A5(I,1) − A5(I,2)
6300      A2 = A2 + A5(I,1) − A5(I,2)
6310    NEXT I
6320    PRINT " **** TOTAL ASSETS"; TAB(36);
6330    PRINT USING F1$; A2
6333    INPUT "CONTINUE"; Z9$
6335    PRINT "   LIABILITIES"
6337    L2 = 0
6340    FOR I = 1+A TO L+A
6350      IF M$(I) = "CLOSED" GOTO 6390
6360      PRINT M$(I); TAB(26);
6370      PRINT USING F1$; A5(I,2) − A5(I,1)
6380      L2 = L2 + A5(I,2) − A5(I,1)
6390    NEXT I
6400    PRINT " **** TOTAL LIABILITIES"; TAB(36);
6410    PRINT USING F1$; L2
6415    PRINT
6420    PRINT "   OWNERS' EQUITY"
6430    O2 = 0
6440    FOR I = A+L+1 TO N
```

Figure 5.13: The Balance Sheet Subroutine (cont.)

```
6450    IF M$(I) = "CLOSED" GOTO 6490
6460    PRINT M$(I); TAB(26);
6470    PRINT USING F1$; A5(I,2) − A5(I,1)
6480      O2 = O2 + A5(I,2) − A5(I,1)
6490    NEXT I
6500    PRINT " ∗∗∗∗ TOTAL OWNERS' EQUITY"; TAB(36);
6510    PRINT USING F1$; O2
6520    PRINT " ∗∗∗∗ TOTAL LIABILITIES PLUS"
6530    PRINT "    OWNERS' EQUITY"; TAB(36);
6540    PRINT USING F1$; L2 + O2
6550    REM
6560    INPUT "CONTINUE"; Z9$
6570    RETURN

9999    END
```

Figure 5.13: The Balance Sheet Subroutine (cont.)

Debugging a Well-Structured Program

At the beginning of this chapter we made the claim that top-down subroutine organization simplifies not only program development and revision, but also debugging. Debugging is, of course, the process of correcting the errors in a program. Program bugs come in two varieties—syntactical and logical. A syntactical bug is a misuse of the programming language itself: misspelling a reserved word; punctuating incorrectly; or failing to adhere perfectly to the strict "grammar" of a programming language. Such bugs are ubiquitous in programming. As Frederick P. Brooks remarks, "Human beings are not accustomed to being perfect . . . Adjusting to the requirement for perfection is, I think, the most difficult part of learning to program."[1]

Fortunately, syntactical errors are usually easy to correct. Many BASIC interpreters provide helpful error messages when a program terminates because of an error in syntax; not only do these messages describe the problem, but they also indicate which line contains the error.

---

[1]Brooks, Frederick P., *The Mythical Man-Month: Essays on Software Engineering.* Reading, Mass.: Addison-Wesley, 1978.

The second variety of bug is more subtle and often much more difficult to correct. *Logical* errors are bugs that do not necessarily cause an abnormal termination of the program, but that produce unexpected and incorrect output from the program. Typical bugs of this kind might be the use of a variable in the wrong place, incorrect implementation of a formula, or execution of a loop a wrong number of times. Generally such bugs appear in exactly the routines that the programmer was certain were perfect. Because most logical bugs are completely unexpected, half the task of correcting them may simply lie in *locating* them in the program.

One technique often used for finding bugs is to generate temporary output messages that describe the current status of the program at any given point during execution. These statements might tell which subroutine is being executed, or what the current value of a certain variable is. For example:

```
2513   PRINT "BEGINNING T—ACCOUNT SUBROUTINE."
2515   PRINT "VALUE OF VARIABLE M3 IS "; M3
```

If statements like these are written for every subroutine of a program, then it can be easier to trace the action of the program and to find the source of a problem. Of course, once the program seems to be running correctly, we would not want these debugging messages to continue appearing. We might simply eliminate them from the program; however, if another problem appears in a later run of the program, then all the error-tracing messages would have to be rewritten.

A simple method exists for preserving these statements so that they are available whenever needed. The debugging statements can be written as part of **IF** statements, so that their execution is dependent on the value of a variable that can be "switched" to true or false. For example:

```
2513   IF D1 THEN PRINT "BEGINNING T-ACCOUNT SUBROUTINE"
```

The value of D1 can be set at the beginning of the program in a sequence such as this:

```
43   D1 = 0 : REM INITIALIZE TO FALSE
45   INPUT "DEBUG (Y OR N)"; A$
47   IF A$ = "Y" THEN D1 = NOT D1 : REM SWITCH TO TRUE
```

Thus, if a whole series of **PRINT** statements displays debugging messages, and if each **PRINT** is prefaced by the phrase **IF** D1, then all these messages can be turned on or off at the beginning of the program run. This can be a permanent tool for debugging a long program throughout the history of its use.

Other Languages

A "structured" COBOL program is organized in blocks of code called sections. Controlling the execution of these sections can be the job of a group of lines at the beginning of the **PROCEDURE DIVISION**. For example:

PROCEDURE DIVISION.

PERFORM 010-HOUSEKEEPING **THRU** 010-HOUSEKEEPING-EXIT.

PERFORM 020-READ-A-CARD **THRU** 020-READ-A-CARD-EXIT
    UNTIL WS-END-OF-FILE = 'A'.

PERFORM 030-HEADING-PRINT **THRU** 030-HEADING-PRINT-EXIT.

PERFORM 040-PRINT-TOTALS **THRU** 040-PRINT-TOTALS-EXIT
    VARYING WS-SUBSCRIPT **FROM** 1 **BY** 1 **UNTIL** WS-SUBSCRIPT > 10.

CLOSE CARD-FILE, PRINT-FILE.

STOP RUN.

This sequence is much like what we have been calling the main program in BASIC. It is followed by the four sections that it "calls," or performs. The sections are named 010-HOUSEKEEPING, 020-READ-A-CARD, 030-HEADING-PRINT, and 040-PRINT-TOTALS. These sections, can, in turn, have **PERFORM** statements that call other sections, in genuine top-down fashion.

The COBOL equivalent of the **ON** statement is **GO TO/ DEPENDING**:

    GO TO
        SALARY
        HOURLY
        SPECIAL-PAYMENT
    DEPENDING ON SALARY-CODE.

This statement branches to one of three sections—SALARY, HOURLY, or SPECIAL-PAYMENT—depending on the value of the variable SALARY-CODE. SALARY-CODE should thus be equal to 1, 2, or 3; if it is out of range, then control passes to the statement following the **GO TO DEPENDING**.

A Pascal subroutine is called a *procedure*:

```
PROCEDURE SALARY      (RATE,
                       PERCENT _ DEDUCT,
                       HOURS         : REAL;
             VAR       GROSSPAY,
                       NETPAY        : REAL);

VAR OVERRATE : REAL;

BEGIN
   IF HOURS > 40.0 THEN
      BEGIN
         HOURS : = HOURS — 40.0;
         OVERRATE : = RATE * 1.5
      END
   ELSE
      OVERRATE : = 0.0;
   GROSSPAY : = (RATE * 40.0) + (HOURS * OVERRATE);
   NETPAY : = GROSSPAY — (GROSSPAY * PERCENT _ DEDUCT)
END; (* SALARY *)
```

The call for this procedure might look something like this:

```
SALARY (HOURLY, TAXRATE, WORKWEEK, GROSS, NET)
```

A procedure call consists of the name of the procedure, and a list of the *parameter* values being passed to that procedure. Notice that the names of the parameters in the procedure call are not the same as the variables in the procedure itself. The variables RATE, PERCENT _ DEDUCT, and HOURS are "dummy parameters," for use in procedure SALARY only. No matter what happens to them, the values of HOURLY, TAXRATE, and WORKWEEK (in the calling program) will remain unchanged. The calculated values of GROSSPAY and NETPAY (listed as **VAR** parameters in procedure SALARY) will be passed back to variables GROSS and NET after SALARY is executed. The variable OVERRATE is a *local* variable, defined and used exclusively in procedure SALARY.

The technique of using local variables is one that is not available in BASIC. With the exception of the dummy parameter in a user-defined function (described in Chapter 6), all BASIC variables are *global*, meaning that every subroutine has access to—and can change the value of—every variable of the program.

Two other Pascal features are similar to BASIC instructions that we have discussed in this chapter. The Pascal **CASE** statement matches the BASIC **ON** statement:

```
CASE MENUCHOICE OF
    1 : TDISPLAY;
    2 : TCHANGE;
    3 : TRIALBALANCE;
    4 : BALSHEET
END;
```

The variable after the word **CASE**—MENUCHOICE, in this example—is called the **CASE** *selector*, and the values of the selector are called the *labels.* Depending on the value of MENUCHOICE, one of four statements can be executed by this **CASE** statement. Here all four statements happen to be subroutine calls; however, any Pascal statement is legal after the **CASE** label.

Like the **ON** statement in BASIC, the **CASE** statement must be used cautiously; if the value of the selector falls outside of the range of the labels, different versions of Pascal react differently.

Finally, Pascal allows us to define variables of type BOOLEAN:

```
VAR
    UNEQUAL : BOOLEAN;
```

BOOLEAN variables have a range of exactly two values: TRUE or FALSE, which are predefined constants in Pascal. The following statements might appear in a Pascal version of our transaction program:

```
UNEQUAL := FALSE;
DCCHECK;                 (* SUBROUTINE CALL FOR DEBIT/CREDIT *)
IF UNEQUAL THEN TCHANGE;
```

(Also note that the symbols (∗ and ∗) allow the programmer to incorporate comments into a Pascal program.)

FORTRAN subroutines also have dummy parameters:

```
        SUBROUTINE DISCNT (NYEARS, ERATE, DISFAC, ANFAC)
        DIMENSION DISFAC(30)
        ANFAC = 0.0
        DO 10 K = 1, NYEARS
        DISFAC(K) = 1.0 / ((1.0 + ERATE / 100.0))**K)
        ANFAC = ANFAC + DISFAC(K)
  10    CONTINUE
        RETURN
        END
```

This subroutine, which computes present value and annuity factors, might be called with a statement like:

```
        CALL DISCNT (5,18,PRESFACS, ANNUITY)
```

The calculated values of the array DISFAC and the variable ANFAC are passed back to PRESFACS and ANNUITY in the main program. Notice the syntax of the subroutine: it must contain both the words **RETURN** and **END** to be complete.

Boolean variables are defined in FORTRAN in the **LOGICAL** statement:

```
        LOGICAL UNEQUAL
```

Logical variables may be assigned one of two constants: .TRUE. or .FALSE..

FORTRAN also provides a **DATA** statement:

```
        DATA ACCOUNTS, ASSETS, LIABILITIES, OEQ / 11, 4, 2, 5 /
```

This statement initializes the four variables with the values that are listed between the slashes.

Summary

We have seen how careful use of subroutines can substantially improve the organization of a BASIC program. Top-down, modular structure allows a program to be written and tested in steps. The use of stubs is a technique of abbreviating or simulating the action of a subroutine until the actual subroutine can be written.

Organizing a program in subroutines can also simplify the debugging process. If each subroutine implements a well-defined and limited task, then the programmer at least has a systematic approach to finding the source of logical errors.

Long BASIC programs are notoriously unreadable; yet this need not be the case. Subroutine structure combined with adequate documentation in the form of **REM** comments can go a long way in making BASIC programs as easy to read and understand as programs in any other language.

Exercises

5.1: Try adding some new accounts to the general ledger program. Remember that only the **DATA** statements (lines 770 to 820) need be revised to add more accounts.

5.2: Add debugging code to each subroutine of the general ledger program, following the suggestion outlined near the end of this chapter.

5.3: Rework the depreciation program of Chapter 4 according to the "structured" programming methods described in this chapter. Draw a structure chart of the new program you will write.

5.4: Outline a plan for generating an income statement from the general ledger program. What new accounts would have to be added? What parts of the income statement program of Chapter 2 could be used for this new procedure?

*5.5: Write a program that supplies options for inventory costing methods (LIFO, FIFO, weighted average). Use the **ON/GOSUB** instruction to create a menu for the program.

5.6: The T-accounts produced by the general ledger program in this chapter actually represent only a summary of the entries for any given account. A more genuine and useful version of the T-account would contain a record of each individual debit or credit to the account. How would you revise the program to improve the usefulness of the T-account presentation?

---

*Answer appears in Appendix A.

CHAPTER 6

Arithmetic Functions

BASIC OFFERS both built-in and user-defined functions. In this chapter we will learn the difference between these two kinds of functions, and we will examine arithmetic applications of both. In Chapter 7 we will study functions that operate on strings.

Three programs will be presented in this chapter. First, a short statistical analysis program will illustrate the use of built-in functions. Then, as an introduction to user-defined functions, we will see how to implement a simple rounding function, and we will use it as a substitute to the **PRINT USING** statement. We will run a test program to compare the results of **PRINT USING** with our rounding function.

Finally, in the break-even point program, we will put these concepts into practice. This program calculates the break-even point in unit sales for a given production category and the target unit sales necessary for a given target net profit. In addition, the program produces a graph of the break-even point.

Built-In Functions

We have already seen examples of two built-in functions in earlier chapters. The **ABS** function appeared in both the income statement program (Chapter 2) and the general ledger program (Chapter 5), and the **INT** function appeared in the monthly sales program (Chapter 3).

Different BASICs supply more or less extensive libraries of built-in functions. Some common arithmetic functions that are available in most BASICs are listed and described in Figure 6.1. The general form

Function		Range of Arguments
Arithmetic		
INT	Truncated Integer Value	real
ABS	Absolute Value	real
SQR	Square Root	nonnegative real
Trigonometric		
SIN	Sine	radians
COS	Cosine	radians
TAN	Tangent	radians
ATN	Arctangent	real
Exponential		
LOG	Natural Logarithm	nonnegative real
EXP	e^x	real
Random Number Generator		
RND	Produces random numbers	implementation-dependent

Figure 6.1: Common BASIC Built-In Functions

of these functions is:

FNAME(A)

where FNAME is the name of the function, and A is the *argument* of the function. The argument may be a variable, an expression, or a number, although range restrictions apply to the arguments of some functions.

The table in Figure 6.2 shows some short test programs illustrating the use of these functions in actual BASIC instructions. Examine this table carefully before proceeding through this chapter.

	BASIC Statement	**Output Results**
10	X = −9.87	Y = 9.87
20	Y = **ABS**(X)	Z = 9
30	**PRINT** "Y = "; Y	S = 3
40	Z = **INT**(Y)	
50	**PRINT** "Z = "; Z	
60	S = **SQR**(Z)	
70	**PRINT** "S = "; S	
110	P = 3.1415926	
120	**PRINT** "SINE OF PI/2 = ";	SINE OF PI/2 = 1
130	**PRINT SIN**(P/2)	COSINE OF PI/2 = 0
140	**PRINT** "COSINE OF PI/2 = ";	
150	**PRINT COS**(P/2)	
210	E = **EXP**(1)	
220	**PRINT** "E = "; E	E = 2.71828
310	**FOR** I = 1 **TO** 5	.768709
320	**PRINT RND**(0)	.781397
330	**NEXT** I	.0767001
		.529509
		.0488598

Figure 6.2: Examples of BASIC Functions

In the statistical analysis program, presented in the next section, we will look in more detail at two of these functions—**RND** and **SQR**.

Statistical Analysis of Random Numbers

Various elements of statistical analysis are used in many business management decision models. Here we will examine three of the simplest and most commonly used calculations—the mean, the variance, and the standard deviation. We will apply these calculations to a series of random numbers that will be generated by our program.

The *mean* of a series of numbers is simply the sum divided by the number of elements in the series. Mathematically this is expressed as:

$$M = \frac{\Sigma N_i}{n}$$

where N_i is the series of numbers and n is the number of elements in the series. (The Greek letter sigma, Σ, signifies summation.)

In BASIC this calculation might look something like this:

```
100   T = 0
110   FOR I = 1 TO N%
120      T = T + N(I)
130   NEXT I
140   M = T/N%
```

The series of numbers is stored in the array N. A **FOR** loop finds the sum of these numbers, and then the average is calculated in line 140.

Given N_i, a series of n numbers, the *variance, V,* is defined as the sum of the squares of the differences between the mean, M, and each number in the series, divided by $n - 1$:

$$V = \frac{\Sigma (M - N_i)^2}{n - 1}$$

The standard deviation, S, is the square root of the variance:

$$S = \sqrt{V}$$

Working again with the array N, we would calculate the variance and standard deviation in BASIC as follows:

```
200   V = 0
210   FOR I = 1 TO N
220      V = V + (M − N(I))^2
230   NEXT I
240   V = V/(N − 1)
250   S = SQR(V)
```

Here the **FOR** loop finds the sum of the squares of the differences between M and N(I). Then the variance and standard deviation are computed in lines 240 and 250. Notice the use of the **SQR** function to find the square root of the variance. Since the argument of **SQR** must be greater than or equal to zero, we would normally want to test the value of V before executing line 250:

```
245   IF V < 0 THEN STOP
```

However, in this case we know that V will not be negative because the expression:

$$(M − N(I))^2$$

is always greater than or equal to zero.

A complete statistical analysis program is shown in Figure 6.3, and the output from this program is shown in Figure 6.4. The program generates a series of random numbers and then performs the statistical analysis calculations on this series. The BASIC random number generator **RND** is used to create the series of numbers. The random numbers are stored in the array R; assignments to the elements of R are made inside a **FOR** loop until N% random numbers have been generated:

```
170   R(I) = RND(0)
```

Both the argument and the results of the **RND** function vary widely in different BASICs. Most BASICs generate random numbers between 0 and 1. In some BASICs, however, the argument can be changed to determine the range and type of random numbers that will be generated. Some BASICs also supply a method of adjusting the starting point of the random number generator to assure an unpredictable sequence of random numbers. This process is referred to as initial-izing the "seed" of the random number generator. It is, of course, important to know the details of the **RND** function for a given BASIC before trying to use the function in a program.

In the next section we will examine user-defined functions, and we will create a rounding function.

```
 10   REM       STATISTICAL ANALYSIS OF RANDOM NUMBERS
 20   REM
 30   REM       VARIABLE NAMES
 40   REM       R                   ARRAY OF RANDOM NUMBERS
 50   REM       T                   TOTAL (SUM) OF NUMBERS
 60   REM       N%                  NUMBER OF RANDOM NUMBERS
 70   REM       M                   MEAN OF RANDOM NUMBERS
 80   REM       V                   VARIANCE
 90   REM       D                   STANDARD DEVIATION
100   REM
110   REM       ADAPTED FROM PASCAL PROGRAMS FOR
115   REM       SCIENTISTS AND ENGINEERS
120   REM       BY A. R. MILLER
125   REM
130   INPUT "HOW MANY RANDOM NUMBERS"; N%
140   DIM R(N%)
150   T = 0
160   FOR I = 1 TO N%
170      R(I) = RND(0)
180      PRINT I, R(I)
190      T = T + R(I)
200   NEXT I
210   M = T/N%
220   V = 0
230   FOR I = 1 TO N%
240      V = V + (M − R(I))^2
250   NEXT I
```

Figure 6.3: Statistical Analysis Program

```
260   PRINT "MEAN = "; M
265   V = V/(N% −1)
270   PRINT "VARIANCE = "; V
280   D = SQR(V)
290   PRINT "STANDARD DEVIATION = "; D
300   END
```

Figure 6.3: Statistical Analysis Program (cont.)

```
HOW MANY RANDOM NUMBERS? 15
1                   .768709
2                   .781397
3                   .0767001
4                   .529509
5                   .0488598
6                   .651496
7                   .493377
8                   .569345
9                   .641721
10                  .953765
11                  .407915
12                  .938538
13                  .14391
14                  .534092
15                  .734801
MEAN =   .551609
VARIANCE =   .080907
STANDARD DEVIATION = .284442
```

Figure 6.4: Output from Statistical Analysis Program

User-Defined Functions

Although BASIC supplies many useful built-in functions, it is often convenient to define new functions that can be *called* whenever they are needed in a program. Most BASICs have the **DEF FN** statement, which allows the user to *define* such new functions. The **DEF** statement takes the following form:

DEF FNA(X) = (function of variable X)

The letters **FN** stand for function, and the letter A is the distinguishing name of the function. **FN** may be followed by any variable name; for example, **FNG, FNM1**, and so on. (Some BASICs also allow definition of string functions such as **FNS$**.)

The variable X in the **DEF** statement is called a *dummy* variable. The value of another variable, say Y, may be "passed" to X so that the value of Y will be used to calculate the value of **FN**A. The best way to see what this means is through an example.

Let us say we wish to round a real number to two decimal places. If the third decimal place contains a digit of 5 or greater, we will round up; if the third decimal place contains a digit of less than 5 we will round down. For example,

> 125.3761

would be rounded to:

> 125.38

On the other hand, the number:

> 946.223

would be rounded down to:

> 946.22

We will use the following algorithm to perform the rounding in BASIC:

1. Multiply the number by 100, so that the first decimal place contains the determining digit for the rounding operation.

2. Add 0.5 to result of step 1. Thus, if the first decimal place is 5 or more, the first digit *before* the decimal will be increased by 1. (If the first decimal place is less than 5, the result will be unchanged.)

3. Take the integral value of the result of step 2, using the **INT** function.

4. Divide the result by 100.

The table in Figure 6.5 illustrates how this algorithm works on the number 125.3761.

We can express this algorithm in BASIC as:

> 10   **DEF FN**R(X) = **INT**(100 * X + 0.5)/100

With the rounding function **FNR** thus defined in our program, we can call the function simply by writing the name of the function and the name of a variable as the argument of the function. For example:

```
15    Y = 125.3761
20    PRINT FNR(Y)
```

Now we can see why the X in the **DEF** statement is called a *dummy* variable. The argument of the call to **FNR** may be any variable, arithmetic expression, or number that we wish to pass to the function. We might, for example, write a complex expression as the argument of **FNR**:

```
40    PRINT FNR(N(I)/15)
```

The argument here is an array element (N(I)) divided by 15.

One obvious use for this particular rounding function is to round monetary values to the nearest cent. Up to now in this book we have used the **PRINT USING** statement to perform rounding. Some BASICs, unfortunately, do not have **PRINT USING**. In its place we could use function **FNR**:

PRINT "$"; FNR(M)

Figure 6.6 lists a program that can be used to compare the results of **PRINT USING** with our user-defined rounding function. The output is shown in Figure 6.7. This test program reads ten real numbers from **DATA** statements and prints them first in the **PRINT**

Step	Description	Result
		125.3761
(1)	* 100	12537.61
(2)	+ .5	12538.11
(3)	INT	12538
(4)	100	125.38

Figure 6.5: Rounding Algorithm

USING format, then in the format produced by the user-defined function. The resulting table allows us to compare the two techniques.

Study the output carefully and note the several advantages of **PRINT USING** over the user-defined function:

1. **PRINT USING** produces a floating dollar sign, which is always directly next to the leftmost digit; some BASICs put a space between the dollar sign and the first digit when the user-defined function is used.

2. **PRINT USING** includes commas in the number.

3. **PRINT USING** aligns the decimal points in a vertical list of numbers; the **FNR** function left-justifies the numbers.

Another disadvantage of the user-defined function is that it does not print ending zeroes to the right of the decimal point. All the same, our function **FNR** is a reasonable alternative if **PRINT USING** is not available.

We will next see a variation of our rounding function and several different applications of it in the break-even point program.

```
 10   REM      TEST PROGRAM TO COMPARE 'PRINT USING' AND
 20   REM      USER—CREATED ROUNDING FUNCTION.
 30   REM      D. HERGERT          19 SEPT 81
 40   REM
 50   DEF FNR(X) = INT(100 * X + 0.5)/100
 60   U$ = "$$##,#####.##"
 70   PRINT "NUMBER", "PRINT USING", "USER—CREATED"
 80   PRINT "– – – – – –", "– – – – – – – – – –", "– – – – – – – – – –"
 90   READ N
100   FOR I = 1 TO N
110      READ M
120      PRINT M,
130      PRINT USING U$; M;
140      PRINT , "$"; FNR(M)
```

Figure 6.6: Test Program

```
150   NEXT I
160   DATA 10
170   DATA 234.567
180   DATA 127.9
190   DATA 12345.987
200   DATA 25562.00
210   DATA 134.8709
220   DATA 1.1
230   DATA 13423.23
240   DATA 6766.66
250   DATA 14545.22
260   DATA 345.66
270   END
```

Figure 6.6: Test Program (cont.)

```
     NUMBER        PRINT USING      USER-CREATED
     ------        -----------      ------------
     234.567          $234.57       $ 234.57
     127.9            $127.90       $ 127.9
     12346         $12,346.00       $ 12346
     25562         $25,562.00       $ 25562
     134.871          $134.87       $ 134.87
     1.1                $1.10       $ 1.1
     13423.2       $13,423.20       $ 13423.2
     6766.66        $6,766.66       $ 6766.66
     14545.2       $14,545.20       $ 14545.2
     345.66           $345.66       $ 345.66
```

Figure 6.7: Output of Test Program

Cost-Volume-Profit Analysis

In determining the break-even point for a given production activity, we distinguish between *fixed costs* and *variable costs*. Fixed costs are the periodic costs that remain the same, independent of the number of units produced (within a "relevant range" of production). Costs that fall into this category are rent, insurance, property tax, and so on. Variable costs are the per-unit production costs of an item. The total variable costs are directly proportional to the number of units produced. Variable costs might include materials, commissions, parts, supplies, and some types of labor.

Thus, the total costs for a given activity are represented by the sum of the applicable fixed costs and the variable costs. If we are discussing production and sales activity, then the total variable costs equal the number of units produced times the variable cost per unit.

The *break-even point* is met when total gross revenues exactly match fixed costs plus variable costs. We can also define the break-even point as the activity level where there is neither a net loss nor a net gain, i.e., the profit equals zero. Figure 6.8 illustrates this concept graphically. The point at which the revenues line intersects with the total costs line is the break-even point.

Before the break-even point, the net loss is represented by the vertical distance between the total costs line and the revenues line. After the break-even point, a net gain is represented by the amount that revenues exceed total costs.

Given the applicable fixed costs, F, the selling price per unit, P, and

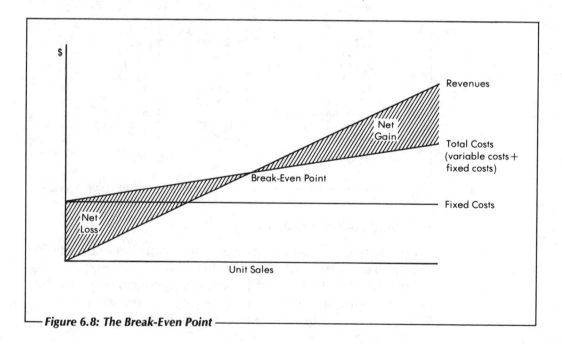

Figure 6.8: The Break-Even Point

the variable costs per unit, C, we can calculate the break-even point in unit sales, B, as follows:

$$B = \frac{F}{P - C} \tag{1}$$

We may also add a figure for the target net profit, T, to this formula, to find the target unit sales, S:

$$S = \frac{F + T}{P - C} \tag{2}$$

The program shown in Figure 6.9 and its accompanying output in Figure 6.10 demonstrate the use of these formulas. This program is actually part of a subroutine for a larger program that we will see in the next section. Equations 1 and 2 are implemented in lines 390 and 430, respectively. Notice also line 400, a variation of our rounding algorithm:

400   **DEF FN**A(X) = **INT**(X + 0.5)

This function is used to round the figures for unit sales to the nearest unit. It is more accurate than using **INT**, which merely truncates decimal values.

In the following section we will look at the entire break-even point program.

```
320   PRINT "NAME OF UNIT";
330   INPUT N$
340   PRINT "COST PER "; N$; " (VARIABLE EXPENSES)";
350   INPUT C
360   PRINT "SELLING PRICE PER "; N$;
370   INPUT P
380   INPUT "FIXED EXPENSES PER PERIOD"; F
390   B = F/(P − C)
400   DEF FNA(X) = INT(X + 0.5)
410   PRINT "BREAK EVEN POINT = "; FNA(B); " "; N$; " SALES"
420   INPUT "TARGET NET PROFIT"; T
430   S = (F + T)/(P − C)
440   PRINT "TARGET SALES = "; FNA(S); " "; N$; " SALES"
```

Figure 6.9: Break-Even Point Calculation Program

```
NAME OF UNIT? WIDGET
COST PER WIDGET (VARIABLE EXPENSES)? 4.50
SELLING PRICE PER WIDGET? 9
FIXED EXPENSES PER PERIOD? 1000
BREAK EVEN POINT =   222   WIDGET SALES
TARGET NET PROFIT? 1000
TARGET SALES =   444   WIDGET SALES
```

Figure 6.10: Output from Break-Even Point Calculation Program

The Break-Even Point Program with Graph

Since cost-volume-profit analysis is in fact a management decision tool, it might be useful to produce a graph of the calculations as part of the output of the program. Furthermore, one run of the program should allow several different analyses for comparison. Figure 6.11 shows the output from such a run. The first part of the output is similar to what we saw in Figure 6.10: a simple input/output dialogue that displays calculations for the break-even point and the target sales. Following this dialogue is a plotted graph, based on the graph in Figure 6.8. This output graph has five lines: the x-and y-axes, (represented by lines of Xs and Ys); the revenues as a function of unit sales (represented by the # symbol); the fixed costs (represented by + symbols); and finally the total costs (represented by * symbols). As in Figure 6.8, the break-even point is the intersection of the total costs line and the revenues line.

The third part of the output is a key to the graph, explaining the meaning of each line, and summarizing the quantities represented by the lines.

Finally, the line:

ANOTHER ANALYSIS (Y OR N)?

appears. At this point, the user may perform the analysis on a different set of data.

The program that produces this output is shown in Figures 6.12 to 6.17. We will discuss each subroutine of the program in turn.

Figure 6.12 displays the main program. The first executable statements (after the variable list) are an assignment statement for D, and a

DIM statement defining the two-dimensional array T$. T$ will hold information for the graph, and D defines the dimensions of the graph. (The size of the graph can thus be adjusted by simply changing the value of D.) Lines 183 and 185 are **DEF** statements for the two rounding functions we will use in the program. Most of the rest of the main program consists of calls to the five subroutines that make up the program. Notice that line 280 loops back to line 200 if the user requests another analysis. The **DIM** and **DEF** statements are located outside of this loop, since they should only be executed once during the run of the program.

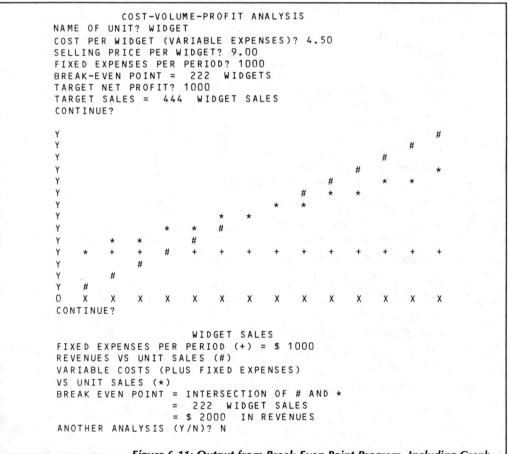

```
                COST-VOLUME-PROFIT ANALYSIS
NAME OF UNIT? WIDGET
COST PER WIDGET (VARIABLE EXPENSES)? 4.50
SELLING PRICE PER WIDGET? 9.00
FIXED EXPENSES PER PERIOD? 1000
BREAK-EVEN POINT =  222   WIDGETS
TARGET NET PROFIT? 1000
TARGET SALES =  444   WIDGET SALES
CONTINUE?

Y                                                            #
Y                                                      #
Y                                                #
Y                                          #
Y                                    #           *     *
Y                              #     *     *
Y                        *     *
Y                  *     *
Y            *     *     #
Y      *     *     #
Y  *   +     +     #     +     +     +     +     +     +     +     +
Y            #
Y      #
Y  #
0  X   X     X     X     X     X     X     X     X     X     X     X     X     X
CONTINUE?

                       WIDGET SALES
FIXED EXPENSES PER PERIOD (+) = $ 1000
REVENUES VS UNIT SALES (#)
VARIABLE COSTS (PLUS FIXED EXPENSES)
VS UNIT SALES (*)
BREAK EVEN POINT = INTERSECTION OF # AND *
                 =  222   WIDGET SALES
                 = $ 2000   IN REVENUES
ANOTHER ANALYSIS (Y/N)? N
```

Figure 6.11: Output from Break-Even Point Program, Including Graph

```
 10   REM        BREAK-EVEN POINT PROGRAM
 20   REM        D. HERGERT            JULY 81
 30   REM
 40   REM        VARIABLE NAMES
 50   REM        N$                    UNIT NAME
 60   REM        C                     VARIABLE COSTS PER UNIT
 70   REM        P                     SELLING PRICE
 80   REM        F                     FIXED EXPENSES PER PERIOD
 90   REM        B                     BREAK-EVEN POINT (IN UNITS SOLD)
100   REM        T                     TARGET NET PROFIT
110   REM        S                     TARGET SALES
120   REM        T$                    TWO-DIMENSIONAL ARRAY FOR GRAPH
130   REM        D                     SIZE OF GRAPH
140   REM
150   REM        MAIN PROGRAM
160   REM
170   D = 14
180   DIM T$(D,D)
183   DEF FNA(X) = INT(X + 0.5)
185   DEF FNB(X) = INT(100 * X + 0.5)/100
190   PRINT TAB(10); "COST-VOLUME-PROFIT ANALYSIS"
200   GOSUB 300 : REM INPUT ROUTINE
210   GOSUB 500 : REM INITIALIZE T$
220   GOSUB 600 : REM COMPUTE LINES OF GRAPH
230   INPUT "CONTINUE"; A$
240   GOSUB 800 : REM PRINT GRAPH
250   INPUT "CONTINUE"; A$
260   GOSUB 900 : REM PRINT KEY TO GRAPH
270   INPUT "ANOTHER ANALYSIS (Y/N)"; A$
280   IF A$ = "Y" GOTO 200
290   GOTO 1080 : REM END
```

Figure 6.12: Break-Even Point: Main Program

The input subroutine, listed in Figure 6.13, is virtually the same as the simple break-even point program we saw earlier. Line 400, formerly a **DEF** statement, has been removed (and relocated in the main program, as we have already seen), and a **RETURN** statement has been added.

The subroutine shown in Figure 6.14 initializes each element of the array T$ to one blank space. We might think of T$ as representing a piece of graph paper that is D squares wide by D squares long. Some of the squares will be filled with the graphics characters that will make up the lines of the graph. When these characters are all assigned to the proper squares (elements of the array), then we will print out the array, line by line, to produce a copy of the graph. It will be important at that point to print a blank space for any array element that contains no graphics character; otherwise the graph would lose its correct proportions, and become distorted.

The initialization of T$ is performed inside a pair of nested **FOR** loops so that all D by D of the "squares" are assigned a blank.

```
300   REM        INPUT SUBROUTINE
310   REM
315   PRINT
320   PRINT "NAME OF UNIT";
330   INPUT N$
340   PRINT "COST PER "; N$; " (VARIABLE EXPENSES)";
350   INPUT C
360   PRINT "SELLING PRICE PER "; N$;
370   INPUT P
380   INPUT "FIXED EXPENSES PER PERIOD"; F
390   B = F/(P − C)
400   REM
410   PRINT "BREAK−EVEN POINT = "; FNA(B); " "; N$; "S"
420   INPUT "TARGET NET PROFIT"; T
430   S = (F + T)/(P − C)
440   PRINT "TARGET SALES = "; FNA(S); " "; N$; " SALES"
450   RETURN
```

Figure 6.13: Break-Even Point: Input Subroutine

The graph subroutine (Figure 6.15) is the heart of the plotting algorithm used in this program. The first thing to notice is that this subroutine produces no output. Its only task is to assign graphics characters to appropriate elements of the array T$.

In the first two executable lines of the subroutine, the variables X1 and Y1 are assigned values. Actually, we should think of X1 and Y1 as constants; they are used to define the *scale* of the graph, that is, the values represented by one "square" of our imaginary piece of graph paper. These values are calculated in terms of S and P. Recall that S is the target sales (in units) for this activity. P * S thus represents the target profit in dollars. We have decided arbitrarily to make the graph S units wide (horizontal axis) by P * S units long (vertical axis). Since the graph itself is D by D in dimension, one square will represent S/D units sold horizontally, and (P * S)/D dollars vertically.

All five lines of the graph are plotted in a **FOR** loop:

    700   **FOR** X = X1 **TO** S **STEP** X1

Thinking again in terms of a piece of graph paper, we can see that this **FOR** loop moves column by column through the entire graph. For each x-value (column), the y-value (row) of each of the lines is determined, and an assignment is made to the appropriate element of the array T$. Notice that the two lines that are neither horizontal nor vertical (i.e., have finite, nonzero slopes) need to be calculated.

```
500   REM      SUBROUTINE TO INITIALIZE T$
510   REM
520   REM      ALL ELEMENTS OF THE ARRAY
530   REM      ARE INITIALIZED TO ONE SPACE
535   REM
540   FOR I = 1 TO D
550      FOR J = 1 TO D
560         T$(I,J) = " "
570      NEXT J
580   NEXT I
590   RETURN
```

Figure 6.14: Break-Even Point: Initialize T$

The total revenues are calculated and then a "#" character is assigned to represent the value on the graph:

```
730   Y = P * X
740   T$(FNA(X/X1),FNA(Y/Y1)) = "#"
```

In the same manner, the total costs are calculated and the "*" character is assigned:

```
760   Y = C * X + F
770   T$(FNA(X/X1),FNA(Y/Y1)) = "*"
```

The **FN**A function is used to round each value to the closest integer to maintain as much accuracy as possible in the graph.

```
600   REM        GRAPH SUBROUTINE
610   REM
620   REM        VARIABLE NAMES
630   REM        X1, Y1              USED TO DETERMINE THE SCALE
640   REM                           OF THE D BY D GRAPH
650   REM        X, Y               ACTUAL VARIABLES USED TO PLOT
660   REM                           LINES OF GRAPH
670   X1 = S/D
680   Y1 = (P * S)/D
690   T$(0,0) = "0"
700   FOR X = X1 TO S STEP X1
710      T$(FNA(X/X1),FNA(F/Y1)) = "+"     : REM    FIXED COSTS
720      T$(FNA(X/X1),0) = "X"             : REM    X-AXIS
730      Y = P * X
740      T$(FNA(X/X1,FNA(Y/Y1)) = "#"      : REM    REVENUES
750      T$(0,FNA(Y/Y1)) = "Y"             : REM    Y-AXIS
760      Y = C * X + F
770      T$(FNA(X/X1),FN(Y/Y1)) = "*"      : REM    TOTAL COSTS
780   NEXT X
790   RETURN
```

Figure 6.15: Break-Even Point: Graph Subroutine

The subroutine in Figure 6.16 prints the graph. The graph is displayed row by row from the maximum value of Y down to zero:

820 **FOR** Y = D **TO** 0 **STEP** −1

and for each row, from 0 to the maximum value of X:

830 **FOR** X = 0 **TO** D

The string B$ puts three spaces between each column of the graph. (This space, like the value of D, can be adjusted for different output media.) Finally, at the end of each row, a **PRINT** statement is executed so that the next row can be started in the proper position.

The last subroutine of the program (Figure 6.17) prints the key to the graph. Notice that this routine uses both the **FNA** rounding function, to print the unit sales of the break-even point, and the **FNB** function, to print the revenues in dollars.

```
800   REM        SUBROUTINE: PRINT GRAPH
810   REM
815   B$ = "   "
820   FOR Y = D TO 0 STEP −1
830      FOR X = 0 TO D
840         PRINT T$(X,Y); B$;
850      NEXT X
860      PRINT
870   NEXT Y
880   RETURN
```

Figure 6.16: Break-Even Point: Graph Output Subroutine

```
900   REM        GRAPH KEY SUBROUTINE
910   REM
920   REM        FUNCTION FNB ROUNDS OFF
930   REM        DOLLAR TOTALS TO NEAREST CENT
940   REM        (FNB LOCATED IN MAIN PROGRAM)
950   REM
960   PRINT TAB(20); N$; " SALES"
```

Figure 6.17: Break-Even Point: Graph Key Subroutine

```
 970   PRINT "FIXED EXPENSES PER PERIOD (+) = ";
 980   PRINT "$"; FNB(F)
 990   PRINT "REVENUES VS UNIT SALES (#)"
1000   PRINT "VARIABLE COSTS (PLUS FIXED EXPENSES)"
1010   PRINT "VS UNIT SALES (*)"
1020   PRINT "BREAK EVEN POINT = INTERSECTION OF # AND *"
1030   PRINT "                  = "; FNA(B); " "; N$; " SALES"
1040   PRINT "                  = $"; FNB(B*P);
1050   PRINT " IN REVENUES "
1060   RETURN
1070   REM
1080   END
```

Figure 6.17: Break-Even Point: Graph Key Subroutine (cont.)

Other Languages

FORTRAN, like BASIC, has one-line, user-defined functions. In FORTRAN, these functions may have multiple dummy variables. For example, the following line defines the function EQ1:

EQ1(A,B,C,X) = A * X**2 + B * X + C

A call to this function might look like this:

Y = EQ1(1,2,1, X1)

where X1 has been assigned a value earlier in the program.

FORTRAN, Pascal, and some "advanced" BASICs also have *multi-line* functions that return a single value to the calling program. A FORTRAN function that will find the *mean* of the elements of an array might be written as follows:

```
      FUNCTION AMEAN (ARY, N)
      DIMENSION ARY(1000)
      TOTAL = 0.0
      DO 100 I = 1, N
      TOTAL = TOTAL + ARY(I)
100   CONTINUE
```

```
                    P = N
                    AMEAN = TOTAL / P
                    RETURN
                    END
```

For an array A that has J elements (J < = 1000) we might write:

```
        X = AMEAN(A, J)
```

Notice that an assignment statement is used to convert the integer N to a real number before the calculation of the average in this function:

```
        P = N
```

The same function in Pascal could be written as follows:

```
        FUNCTION MEAN (A : ARY; (* ARRAY OF VALUES *)
                       NUM : INTEGER (* NUMBER OF VALUES *)
                       ): REAL;

        VAR
            I    : INTEGER;
            SUM : REAL;

        BEGIN
            SUM : = 0.0;
            FOR I : = 1 TO NUM
                SUM : =SUM + A[I];
            MEAN : = SUM / NUM
        END;
```

The type ARY would have to be defined in the main program heading:

```
        TYPE
            ARY = ARRAY[1..N] OF REAL;
```

A call to this function might appear as:

```
        M : = MEAN(A1,N);
```

In an advanced BASIC that allows multi-line user-defined functions, the word **FNEND** is used to indicate the end of the function, as in the following lines:

```
100   DEF FNA(X)
110   FNA = 0
120   IF X < 0 GOTO 140
130   FNA = SQR(2 * X + 5)
140   FNEND
```

This function returns a value of 0 if the argument is less than 0. For positive or 0 arguments, the function returns the square root of (2X + 5).

Summary

In this chapter we have seen how to make use of both built-in and user-defined functions for numeric applications. We have also seen a number of interesting programs, including one that presents a graph for cost-volume-profit analysis.

While we have limited ourselves to simple rounding functions in our user-defined function examples, it should be clear that functions can be useful for many different applications. The exercises for this chapter offer several more examples of user-created functions.

Exercises

6.1: *Revise the break-even point calculation program (Figure 6.9) to find the target sales for a given target after-tax net income. Add an* **INPUT** *line for the tax rate. Note the following formula:*

$$\text{income before taxes} = \frac{\text{after-tax net income}}{1 - \text{tax rate}}$$

6.2: *On a profit-volume graph the horizontal axis represents volume in units, and the vertical axis represents net income. The profit-volume line crosses the horizontal axis at the break-even point, i.e., the point where net income equals zero; the line crosses the vertical axis at a negative point equal to the fixed costs. The slope of the profit-volume line is equal to the* unit contribution margin, *the difference between the selling price and the variable costs. Write a subroutine to produce such a graph and incorporate it into the break-even point program in place of the subroutine at line 600 (Figure 6.15). Try to replace the "X" and "Y" characters (which make up the horizontal and vertical axes) with numerical values. Rewrite the graph key subroutine (Figure 6.17).*

*6.3: *In some BASICs the range of numbers produced by the* **RND** *function can be defined by the argument of the function. For example,* **RND**(1000) *would produce a random number between 1 and 1000. Write a procedure that produces random numbers between two given integers A and B using an* **RND** *function that returns numbers between 0 and 1.*

*6.4: *The BASIC trigonometric functions deal in radians rather than degrees.* **SIN**, **COS**, *and* **TAN** *take arguments in radians, and* **ATN** *produces results in radians. The following program produces conversion factors between radians and degrees.*

```
10   P = 3.14159
20   R = 2 * P / 360
30   D = 1 / R
40   PRINT "ONE RADIAN = "; D; "DEGREES"
50   PRINT "ONE DEGREE = "; R; "RADIANS"
```

Study this program, run it, and explain how it works. Use the conversion factors it produces to write two user-defined functions—one to convert from radians to degrees, and one to convert from degrees to radians. Then write procedures for the following:

a) the user inputs a number of degrees, and the procedure produces the corresponding **SIN, COS,** and **TAN**.

b) the user inputs a real number, and the procedure produces the corresponding **ATN** in degrees.

6.5: The following program produces a graph of a parabola:

```
10   DEF FNA(X) = X^2
20   FOR I = −10 TO 10
30      PRINT TAB(INT(1 + FNA(I)/30)); "*"
40   NEXT I
50   END
```

Run the program, and explain how it works. What is the equation of the parabola it produces?

---

* Answer appears in Appendix A.

CHAPTER 7

Strings

IN ADDITION TO the arithmetic functions that we discussed in Chapter 6, BASIC offers a variety of built-in functions that operate on strings, or that supply information about strings. In this chapter we will look at a sampling of these functions.

We will begin with a brief description of the ASCII code and the functions **ASC** and **CHR$**. Two programs will be presented for exploring the ASCII code; these programs will also illustrate the **LEN** and **INKEY$** (or **GET**) functions. We will also look at the functions **LEFT$**, **RIGHT$**, and **MID$**.

Finally, we will see an implementation of the simplest of the common sorting algorithms, the *bubble sort*. A sort program is used to put a list of numbers or alphanumeric strings in order. In the personnel list program of this chapter we will see how to alphabetize a list of names.

The ASCII Code

ASCII, the *American Standard Code for Information Interchange,* is used to translate between alphanumeric or special characters and their binary number equivalents specified by the code. Microcomputers commonly use an eight-bit version of ASCII, meaning that each element of the code is represented by an eight-digit binary number, from 00000000 to 11111111. The decimal equivalents of these codes range from 0 to 255; thus, there are 256 elements in an eight-bit ASCII code.

We have noted throughout this book that some features of BASIC differ in the way they are implemented in different versions of the language. The ASCII code is no exception, but some of the 256 elements of the code are relatively "standard." Codes 65 to 90 are the upper-case letters, A to Z; codes 48 to 57 are the digits, 0 to 9. The space character translates into 32, and 33 to 47 are special characters.

For the codes that fall outside the range of 32 to 90, there is considerable variety in the representations. Some BASICs use the upper range of the ASCII code for special graphics characters. Others implement lower-case letters in the upper range of the code.

BASIC supplies two functions that allow the programmer to translate back and forth between the ASCII code numbers (in decimal form) and the characters represented by the code. These functions are **CHR$** and **ASC**, and we will see how they work in the following section.

Two Programs for Exploring ASCII

The argument of the **CHR$** function must be an integer from 0 to 255; the function returns the character represented by the corresponding ASCII code number. The ASCII code program, listed in Figure 7.1, illustrates the use of this function. The output from this program (Figure 7.2) is a table of ASCII code representations from 33 to 95. The **CHR$** function is called in lines 100 to 120, inside a **FOR** loop, to produce the table.

CHR$** can be used to produce characters that cannot be entered from the keyboard (for example, the graphics characters). Another common use of **CHR$ is to produce the double quote character in an

```
10    REM        ASCII CODE PROGRAM
20    REM        D. HERGERT        27 SEPT 81
30    REM
40    S$ = "ASCII  CODE"
50    L = 40
60    PRINT : PRINT : PRINT
70    PRINT TAB((L−LEN(S$))/2); S$
80    PRINT
90    FOR I = 33 TO 53
100       PRINT I; " "; CHR$(I),
110       PRINT I + 21; " "; CHR$(I+21),
120       PRINT I + 42; " "; CHR$(I+42)
130    NEXT I
140    END
```

Figure 7.1: The ASCII Code Program

```
                        ASCII CODE

        33   !           54   6           75   K
        34   "           55   7           76   L
        35   #           56   8           77   M
        36   $           57   9           78   N
        37   %           58   :           79   O
        38   &           59   ;           80   P
        39   '           60   <           81   Q
        40   (           61   =           82   R
        41   )           62   >           83   S
        42   *           63   ?           84   T
        43   +           64   @           85   U
        44   ,           65   A           86   V
        45   −           66   B           87   W
        46   .           67   C           88   X
        47   /           68   D           89   Y
        48   0           69   E           90   Z
        49   1           70   F           91   [
        50   2           71   G           92   \
        51   3           72   H           93   ]
        52   4           73   I           94   ^
        53   5           74   J           95   _
```

Figure 7.2: Output from ASCII Code Program

output string. BASIC supplies no direct way to do this. The ASCII code 34 represents the double quote; thus, **CHR$**(34) returns this character, as illustrated in the following lines:

```
10   Q$ = CHR$(34)
20   PRINT "THE "; Q$; "ASCII"; Q$; " CODE"
```

The output from this **PRINT** statement is:

```
THE "ASCII" CODE
```

The ASCII code program illustrates another common string function—**LEN**. This function takes a string as its argument, and returns an integer representing the *length,* in characters, of the string. In our program, this function is used to center the title of the table:

```
70   PRINT TAB((L−LEN(S$))/2); S$
```

This formula works for any string S$ that we wish to center over L columns of output. (It is roughly equivalent to tabbing to the center column on a typewriter and then back-spacing once for every two characters of a title that is to be centered.)

The program listed in Figure 7.3 produces the ASCII code for any character that is input from the keyboard. It uses the function **ASC** to translate a character, S$, into its ASCII code equivalent:

```
60   PRINT "THE ASCII CODE FOR "; S$;
70   PRINT " IS "; ASC(S$)
```

The sample output from this program is shown in Figure 7.4. Notice that the input characters do not appear in this dialogue. This is because the **INPUT** statement has not been used in this program; instead, we see an illustration of the **INKEY$** statement:

```
30   S$ = INKEY$
40   IF S$ = "" GOTO 30
```

Each time the **INKEY$** statement is executed, the keyboard is scanned to see if any key has been pressed. If a key has been pressed, **INKEY$** returns the character represented by the key; if not, **INKEY$** returns a *null,* or empty, string. The value returned by **INKEY$** is not echoed on the screen or other output device. Since **INKEY$** is executed in a very short time, it is almost always written inside a loop, as illustrated in our program. The loop continues as long as **INKEY\$** returns a null string (S\$ = '''').

Some BASICs have the **GET** function instead of **INKEY\$**. **GET** is implemented in one of two ways. It may work in a manner similar to **INKEY\$**, scanning the keyboard once each time it is executed:

```
30   GET S$
40   IF S$ = '''' GOTO 30
```

```
10   REM      INKEY$/GET PROGRAM
20   REM
30   S$ = INKEY$ : REM 'GET S$' FOR SOME BASICS.
40   IF S$ = '''' GOTO 30 : REM LOOP MAY NOT BE NECESSARY
50   REM                        IN SOME BASICS.
60   PRINT "THE ASCII CODE FOR "; S$;
70   PRINT " IS "; ASC(S$) : PRINT
80   GOTO 30
```

Figure 7.3: INKEY\$/GET Test Program

```
THE ASCII CODE FOR B IS   66

THE ASCII CODE FOR A IS   65

THE ASCII CODE FOR S IS   83

THE ASCII CODE FOR I IS   73

THE ASCII CODE FOR C IS   67

THE ASCII CODE FOR & IS   38

THE ASCII CODE FOR # IS   35

THE ASCII CODE FOR + IS   43

THE ASCII CODE FOR < IS   60

THE ASCII CODE FOR [ IS   91

THE ASCII CODE FOR ! IS   33
```

Figure 7.4: Output from INKEY\$/GET Program

Another implementation of **GET** "waits" for the user to input a character; the loop is therefore not necessary:

```
30    GET S$
40    REM       NO LOOP NEEDED.
```

Other String Functions

In this section we will study the functions **LEFT$**, **RIGHT$**, and **MID$**, and present the major program example of this chapter.

The **MID$** function takes three arguments—a string, and two integers:

```
MID$(S$,N,M)
```

**MID$** returns M characters of the string S$, starting from the Nth character. For example, the lines:

```
10    S$ = "ASSETS LIABILITIES OWNERS' EQUITY"
20    PRINT MID$(S$,8,11)
```

produce the output:

```
LIABILITIES
```

LEFT$** and **RIGHT$ both take two arguments, a string and an integer. They return a string of length N:

```
L$ = LEFT$(S$,N)
R$ = RIGHT$(S$,N)
```

As their names imply, **LEFT$** returns the first N characters of the string S$ and **RIGHT$** returns the last N characters of the string S$.

LEFT$ is commonly used to test for a YES or NO input. Previously we have written such tests as follows:

```
10    INPUT "QUESTION (YES OR NO)"; A$
20    IF (A$ = "YES") OR ("A$ = "Y") THEN GOTO 50
```

With the **LEFT$** function we can simplify this test:

```
10    INPUT "QUESTION (YES OR NO)"; A$
20    IF LEFT$(A$,1) = "Y" THEN GOTO 50
```

The **LEFT$** function in line 20 returns the first character of the input string A$. If this character is a Y (meaning, presumably, that the user has typed either Y or YES) then the **GOTO** is executed.

The personnel list program, shown in Figure 7.5, makes use of the **LEFT$** function in two ways. This program produces a list of the employees of a company, and then produces an alphabetized telephone directory. The user may choose to display one or both of these lists; the YES or NO answer is tested with the **LEFT$** function in lines 190 and 220.

The subroutine that prints the telephone directory shows a second use of **LEFT$**. It prints the last names, and the initials of first names of the individuals on the list. The last names are stored in the array L$, the first names in the array F$, and the telephone numbers in the array T$:

```
1270   PRINT " "; L$(I); ", "; LEFT$(F$(I),1); "."; TAB(25); T$(I)
```

The results of this line are shown in the second half of the output from this program (Figure 7.6).

```
10    REM      PERSONNEL LIST PROGRAM
20    REM      D. HERGERT          SEPT 81
25    REM      ADAPTED FROM J.P. LAMOITIER,
30    REM      FIFTY BASIC EXERCISES
35    REM
40    REM      VARIABLE NAMES
50    REM      N                   NUMBER OF NAMES ON LIST
60    REM      L$(N)               ARRAY OF LAST NAMES
70    REM      F$(N)               ARRAY OF FIRST NAMES
80    REM      P$(N)               ARRAY OF POSITIONS
90    REM      T$(N)               ARRAY OF TELEPHONE NUMBERS
100   REM      H$                  HOLDING VARIABLE FOR SORT
110   REM      I, J                LOOP INDICES
120   REM
```

Figure 7.5: Personnel List Program

```
130   REM        MAIN PROGRAM
140   REM
150   READ N
160   DIM L$(N), F$(N), P$(N), T$(N)
170   GOSUB 400 : REM READ DATA
175   PRINT : PRINT : PRINT
180   INPUT "DO YOU WANT A PERSONNEL LIST"; A$
190   IF LEFT$(A$, 1) = "Y" THEN GOSUB 500
200   PRINT : PRINT : PRINT
210   INPUT "DO YOU WANT A TELEPHONE DIRECTORY"; A$
220   IF LEFT$(A$, 1) = "N" THEN GOTO 9999
230   GOSUB 700 : REM SORT LIST
235   PRINT : PRINT : PRINT
240   GOSUB 1200 : REM PRINT SORTED LIST
250   GOTO 9999

400   REM        READ DATA SUBROUTINE
410   REM
420   FOR I = 1 TO N
430      READ L$(I), F$(I), P$(I), T$(I)
440   NEXT I
450   RETURN

500   REM        PRINT PERSONNEL LIST
510   REM
520   PRINT "---------------------------------------"
530   PRINT "   NAME                    POSITION    "
540   PRINT "---------------------------------------"
545   PRINT
550   FOR I = 1 TO N
560      PRINT F$(I); " "; L$(I); TAB(25); P$(I)
570   NEXT I
580   PRINT "---------------------------------------"
590   RETURN
```

Figure 7.5: Personnel List Program (cont.)

```
700   REM      SORT SUBROUTINE
710   REM      SORTS ON LAST NAME
720   REM      USING BUBBLE SORT ALGORITHM
730   REM
740   FOR I = 1 TO N − 1
750     FOR J = I + 1 TO N
760       IF L$(I) > L$(J) THEN GOSUB 800 : REM SWAP
770     NEXT J
780   NEXT I
790   RETURN

800   REM      SWAP ROUTINE
810   REM      SWAPS LAST NAME, FIRST NAME, POSITION,
815   REM      AND PHONE NUMBER
820   REM
830   H$ = L$(I)        : REM LAST NAMES
840   L$(I) = L$(J)
850   L$(J) = H$
860   H$ = F$(I)        : REM FIRST NAMES
870   F$(I) = F$(J)
880   F$(J) = H$
890   H$ = P$(I)        : REM POSITIONS
900   P$(I) = P$(J)
910   P$(J) = H$
920   H$ = T$(I)        : REM TELEPHONE NUMBERS
930   T$(I) = T$(J)
940   T$(J) = H$
950   RETURN

1200  REM      PRINT TELEPHONE LIST
1210  REM
1220  PRINT "---------------------------------------------"
1230  PRINT "   NAME                    TELEPHONE  #      "
1240  PRINT "---------------------------------------------"
1250  PRINT
```

Figure 7.5: Personnel List Program (cont.)

```
1260    FOR I = 1 TO N
1270       PRINT " "; L$(I); ",  "; LEFT$(F$(I),1); "."; TAB(25); T$(I)
1280    NEXT I
1290    PRINT "---------------------------------------------"
1300    RETURN


1990    DATA 12
2000    DATA SHEPARD, CLARA, PRESIDENT, 525 — 6678
2010    DATA INEZ, ROBERT, VICE PRESIDENT, 544 — 9215
2020    DATA SCULLY, LEE, PRODUCTION MGR., 635 — 4711
2030    DATA ALSTON, LOIS, MKTING/ADV., 525 — 7722
2040    DATA GIBSON, DONALD, ACCOUNTING, 635 — 4498
2050    DATA DUFF, JOANNE, SHIPPING/RCVING, 428 — 9711
2060    DATA TIBBS, DANIEL, PRODUCTION STAFF, 625 — 4313
2070    DATA RACHEL, BEN, PRODUCTION STAFF, 525 — 1128
2080    DATA WINTERS, LENA, RECEPTIONIST, 525 — 4233
2090    DATA BENNET, ISABEL, CLERICAL, 544 — 7968
2100    DATA LARSON, DAVID, CLERICAL, 525 — 3819
2110    DATA RYAN, LOUISE, CLERICAL, 525 — 7251


9999    END
```

Figure 7.5: Personnel List Program (cont.)

Let us examine this program in detail. The main program begins by reading the number of employees from the first **DATA** statement (located at line 1990). It then uses this number to set the dimensions of arrays L$, F$, P$, and T$. (P$ represents the position held by each employee.) Then the subroutine at line 400 is called to read the employee information from the remaining **DATA** statements. The subroutine at line 500 prints the personnel list in the order that it was read from the **DATA** statements. The subroutine at line 1200 also prints the list, in a different form, but not until the list has been *sorted* by the bubble sort subroutines (lines 700 to 790 and 800 to 950).

The sort subroutines contain the most interesting algorithm of this program. The bubble sort is the simplest (but not always the most efficient) of several commonly used sorting algorithms. The heart of the algorithm is contained within the nested loops of lines 740 to 780. Each last name in the list is compared, one by one, with each of the

```
DO YOU WANT A PERSONNEL LIST? Y


------------------------------------------
    NAME                    POSITION
------------------------------------------


    CLARA SHEPARD           PRESIDENT
    ROBERT INEZ             VICE PRESIDENT
    LEE SCULLY              PRODUCTION MGR.
    LOIS ALSTON             MKTING/ADV.
    DONALD GIBSON           ACCOUNTING
    JOANNE DUFF             SHIPPING/RCVING
    DANIEL TIBBS            PRODUCTION STAFF
    BEN RACHEL              PRODUCTION STAFF
    LENA WINTERS            RECEPTIONIST
    ISABEL BENNET           CLERICAL
    DAVID LARSON            CLERICAL
    LOUISE RYAN             CLERICAL
------------------------------------------


DO YOU WANT A TELEPHONE DIRECTORY? Y


------------------------------------------
    NAME                    TELEPHONE #
------------------------------------------


    ALSTON, L.              525-7722
    BENNET, I.              544-7968
    DUFF, J.                428-9711
    GIBSON, D.              635-4498
    INEZ, R.                544-9215
    LARSON, D.              525-3819
    RACHEL, B.              525-1128
    RYAN, L.                525-7251
    SCULLY, L.              635-4711
    SHEPARD, C.             525-6678
    TIBBS, D.               625-4313
    WINTERS, L.             525-4233
------------------------------------------
```

Figure 7.6: Output from Personnel List Program

other last names in the list. For each pair of names, if the first name is "greater than" the second name, then the positions of the two names must be swapped:

760   **IF** L$(I) > L$(J) **THEN GOSUB** 800 : **REM** SWAP

It might seem surprising at first that the inequality operations can be used on strings. However, the comparison is actually of the ASCII codes of the corresponding characters of the two strings in any given pair. Thus, if the names:

SHEPARD

and

SCULLY

are compared, the second name will be "less than" the first name, because the ASCII code number for C is lower than the ASCII code number for H.

Once two names are found to be out of order, we need some method of correcting the order. This is the task of the swap subroutine at line 800. The algorithm is fairly simple. The first of the two names is placed in a "holding variable":

830   H$ = L$(I)

The second name is then placed in the position that the first name held:

840   L$(I) = L$(J)

And, finally, the first name, stored in the holding variable, is placed in the former position of the second name:

850   L$(J) = H$

This swapping procedure is performed on all four of the data items that have been recorded for each employee (lines 860 to 940).

This program could be expanded to include other information about employees: salary data, insurance, vacation days, work records, etc. In an actual application the data would probably be stored on a separate disk file, rather than in **DATA** statements in the program itself. However, for a short list, the **DATA** statements are an efficient alternative to the complexities of file management in BASIC.

Other Languages

In the context of this chapter, it is interesting to note that COBOL has its own built-in **SORT** implementation. This is not surprising, as sorting is one of the most common applications of business data processing. The COBOL **SORT** allows ascending (low to high) or descending (high to low) sorts on multiple *keys*. The sort key is the record that the **SORT** operates on. (In COBOL we refer to *major*, or *primary*, and *minor*, or *secondary*, sort keys.)

Summary

In addition to examining several BASIC string functions in this chapter, we have seen one example of an often-used algorithm in business programming—the sort. While the bubble sort is not as efficient as other sorting algorithms for very long lists, it is very easy to program for any application. The bubble sort, can, of course, be used on numeric data as well as string data, as is suggested by the exercises for this chapter.

Exercises

7.1: Revise the ASCII code program (Figure 7.1) to explore the entire range of the code for your BASIC.

7.2: If your BASIC has graphics characters in the upper range of the ASCII code, find an appropriate character to build a bar graph and revise the monthly sales program (of Chapter 3) to use this character.

7.3: Use the "centering" algorithm (line 70, Figure 7.1) to print your name and address centered on the screen of your computer. Adjust the value of L appropriately.

7.4: Add two more pieces of information to the DATA statements of the personnel list program: home address (a string), and office telephone extension number. Revise the subroutine at line 400 to read this information, and devise a way of printing addresses for the employees in the telephone list created by the subroutine at line 1200.

7.5: Add subroutines to produce a third list: sort using the office extension numbers as keys (Exercise 7.4), and produce a list of the employees arranged in order of these numbers.

7.6: Add code to the sort subroutine (lines 700 to 790, Figure 7.5) to insure that two people with the same last name will be arranged according to their first names. Add some names to the DATA statements to test your new code.

---

*Answer appears in Appendix A.

APPENDIX A

Answers to Selected Exercises

THE EXERCISES ANSWERED in this appendix are those that were marked with an asterisk (*) at the end of each chapter. Most of the remaining exercises can, of course, be answered by rereading the appropriate passages and perhaps trying out different solutions on your computer; some exercises can only be answered by seeing how your implementation of BASIC handles a particular situation.

Included in this appendix are two complete programs. One (3.6) is a revision of the monthly sales program to produce a bar graph using separate symbols for cash and credit sales; the other (5.5) is a completely new program that offers a user the option of costing inventory under three different methods. This inventory program merits careful study.

1.1: *listing:* a display (printed or on a screen) of all the lines of a program.

reserved word: a word that is part of a programming language.

interactive: refers to a computer system or program with which the user has a dialogue; each entry by the user can cause a response by the system.

high-level language: a programming language that has powerful instructions expressed in what resembles "natural language"; examples: BASIC, COBOL, Pascal, FORTRAN.

machine language: a set of binary codes representing the memory configurations that can be directly executed by the processor as instructions.

interpreter: a translation program used to carry out statements expressed in a high-level language; an interpreter translates each statement and executes it immediately. Interpreted programs are much slower than compiled ones because a statement must be translated each time it is executed.

compiler: a translation program that converts high-level instructions into a set of binary instructions (object code) for direct processor execution. A compiler translates the complete program once, yielding object code that may then be executed repeatedly.

bug: a mistake in a program. Debugging is the process of correcting these mistakes.

Note: Some of these definitions are adapted from the *International Microcomputer Dictionary* (Sybex: 1981).

1.4: These lines give the user the option of looping back to the beginning of the program and running the COGS calculations on another set of data.

3.3: Add the following two lines to the program:

```
225   FOR K% = 1 TO 2
      ...
255   NEXT K%
```

3.6: Revise the program as follows:

```
130   PRINT "MONTHLY SALES STATISTICS"
140   PRINT
```

```
150   INPUT "NUMBER OF MONTHS"; N%
160   REM
170   PRINT "UNITS REPRESENTED BY ONE BAR GRAPH CHARACTER";
180   INPUT U
190   PRINT "INPUT MONTH, NUMBER OF CASH SALES, NUMBER OF CREDIT SALES"
200   U2 = 0 : U4 = 0
210   FOR I% = 1 TO N%
220     INPUT M$, U1, U3
230     FOR J% = 1 TO INT(U1/U)
240       PRINT "*";
250     NEXT J%
255     FOR K% = 1 TO INT(U3/U)
260       PRINT "#";
265     NEXT K%
267     PRINT
270     U2 = U2 + U1 : U4 = U4 + U3
280   NEXT I%
290   PRINT
300   PRINT "TOTAL CASH SALES IN "; N%; " MONTHS = "; U2
310   PRINT "TOTAL CREDIT SALES IN "; N%; " MONTHS = "; U4
320   PRINT "AVERAGE NUMBER OF UNITS SOLD PER MONTH = "; (U2 + U4)/N%
330   END
```

4.2: The loop in lines 2030 to 2050 takes the place of the exponentiation operation:

```
2010   A = 0
2020   FOR I = 1 TO N
2025     X = 1
2030     FOR J = 1 TO I
2040       X = X * (1/(1+R/100))
2050     NEXT J
2060     D(I) = X
2070     A = A + D(I)
2080   NEXT I
2090   RETURN
```

4.3: Replace lines 3010 to 3040 with the line:

    3010   D2 = N * (N + 1)/2

5.5: Inventory costing program:

```
 10  REM              INVENTORY COSTING METHODS
 20  REM              LIFO, FIFO, OR WEIGHTED AVERAGE
 30  REM
 40  DIM U(25), C(25)
 42  REM
 45  REM              INPUT ROUTINE
 47  REM
 50  INPUT "NUMBER OF PURCHASES"; P1
 60  T1 = 0
 70  T2 = 0
 80  FOR I = 1 TO P1
 90    PRINT "PURCHASE"; I; ": NUMBER OF UNITS";
100    INPUT U(I)
110    T1 = T1 + U(I)
120    PRINT "PURCHASE"; I; ": COST PER UNIT";
130    INPUT C(I)
140    T2 = T2 + C(I) * U(I)
150  NEXT I
160  REM
170  INPUT "NUMBER OF UNITS SOLD"; S1
175  REM
180  REM              MENU
185  REM
190  PRINT "SELECT INVENTORY COSTING METHOD"
200  PRINT "(1) WEIGHTED AVERAGE"
210  PRINT "(2) LIFO"
220  PRINT "(3) FIFO"
230  INPUT "METHOD 1, 2, OR 3"; M%
240  IF (M% <> 1) AND (M% <> 2) AND (M% <> 3) GOTO 230
241  PRINT : PRINT
```

```
243    PRINT T1; "UNITS AVAILABLE FOR SALE, FOR A TOTAL VALUE OF"
245    PRINT USING "$$##,####.##"; T2
247    PRINT : PRINT
250    ON M% GOSUB 1000, 2000, 3000
255    PRINT : PRINT
260    INPUT "ANOTHER COSTING METHOD"; A$
270    IF (A$ = "Y") OR (A$ = "YES") THEN 190
280    GOTO 9999
1000   REM
1010   REM                 WEIGHTED AVERAGE METHOD
1020   REM
1030   A1 = T2/T1
1040   PRINT USING "AVERAGE UNIT COST = $$####.##"; A1
1060   C1 = S1 * A1
1070   PRINT USING "COST OF GOODS SOLD = $$##,#####.##"; C1
1080   PRINT USING "ENDING INVENTORY   = $$##,#####.##"; T2 − C1
1090   RETURN
2000   REM
2010   REM                 LIFO METHOD
2020   REM
2030   H1 = S1
2035   C1 = 0
2040   FOR I = P1 TO 1 STEP −1
2050     IF (H1 < U(I)) THEN 2090
2060     C1 = C1 + U(I) * C(I)
2070     H1 = H1 − U(I)
2080     GOTO 2110
2090     C1 = C1 + H1 * C(I)
2100     H1 = 0
2110   NEXT I
2120   PRINT USING "COST OF GOODS SOLD = $$##,#####.##"; C1
2130   PRINT T1 − S1; " UNITS REMAINING IN INVENTORY, "
2140   PRINT USING "FOR A TOTAL ENDING INVENTORY OF $$##,#####.##"; T2 − C1
2150   RETURN
3000   REM
```

```
3010  REM              FIFO METHOD
3020  REM
3030  H1 = S1
3040  C1 = 0
3050  FOR I = 1 TO P1
3060     IF (H1< U(I)) THEN 3100
3070     C1 = C1 + U(I) * C(I)
3080     H1 = H1 − U(I)
3090     GOTO 3120
3100     C1 = C1 + H1 * C(I)
3110     H1 = 0
3120  NEXT I
3130  PRINT USING "COST OF GOODS SOLD = $$##,#####.##"; C1
3140  PRINT T1 − S1; " UNITS REMAINING IN INVENTORY,"
3150  PRINT USING "FOR A TOTAL ENDING INVENTORY OF $$##,#####.##"; T2 − C1
3160  RETURN
9999  END
```

6.3: The following program produces N random numbers between A and B, given a random number generator, **RND**(0), that returns numbers between 0 and 1. The values N, A, and B are input by the user.

```
10   PRINT "RANDOM NUMBERS"
20   PRINT
30   INPUT "BETWEEN WHAT TWO INTEGERS (MIN, MAX)"; A, B
40   INPUT "HOW MANY RANDOM NUMBERS"; N
50   FOR I = 1 TO N
60      PRINT A + ((B − A) * RND(0))
70   NEXT I
80   END
```

6.4(a):

```
10   PRINT "SIN, COS, AND TAN FROM DEGREES"
15   DEF FNR(X) = X * .0174533
20   PRINT
30   INPUT "DEGREES"; D
40   PRINT "SINE = "; SIN(FNR(D))
```

```
50    PRINT "COSINE = "; COS(FNR(D))
60    PRINT "TANGENT = "; TAN(FNR(D))
70    END
```

6.4(b):

```
10    PRINT "ARCTANGENT IN DEGREES"
20    DEF FND(X) = X * 57.2958
30    PRINT
40    INPUT "TANGENT"; T
50    PRINT "ARCTANGENT = "; FND(ATN(T))
60    END
```

7.6: Add the following three lines to the subroutine:

```
752   IF L$(I) <> L$(J) THEN 760
754   IF F$(I) > F$(J) THEN GOSUB 800 : REM SORT BY FIRST NAME
756   GOTO 770
```

APPENDIX B

Complete Programs in COBOL, Pascal, and FORTRAN

THE THREE PROGRAMS presented in this appendix illustrate much of the syntax that has been described under the headings "Other Languages." Each program can be profitably compared to the BASIC program or subroutine in this book that performs a similar function. These programs, like the BASIC programs presented throughout the book, are accompanied by brief explanations and by samples of program output.

For further reading, the Bibliography contains references to some excellent introductions to these three languages.

COBOL

The COBOL "Invoices" program is designed to read 80-column punched data cards containing invoice information. Each data card describes one sale, and records eight pieces of information about the sale:

1. the invoice number

2. the store branch number

3. the salesperson number

4. the customer number

5. the quantity sold of the item

6. a description of the item

7. the item number

8. the unit price of the item

The program computes the total amount of each sale (i.e., the unit price times the quantity sold), the total for each invoice number, and the total amount of all the invoices recorded. The program also produces an invoice report that "echoes" the information read from the cards, and prints all the computed totals. The output from the program resembles the table shown in Figure B.1. Since most of this program is devoted to writing the report, it should be compared to programs like the comparative income statement program (Chapter 2) and the balance sheet subroutine (Chapter 5).

The listing of the COBOL program appears in Figure B.2. Note the four divisions of the program. The **IDENTIFICATION DIVISION** records information about the program—title, author, date, etc. The **ENVIRONMENT DIVISION** identifies the computer(s) that will be used to compile and execute the program, and, in the **SELECT** statements, associates the input and output files with the appropriate devices (in this case a card reader and a printer).

The **DATA DIVISION** defines the structure of the input and output files and identifies other, intermediate data structures that will be used in the program. The **FILE SECTION** contains an **FD** (file description) statement for each of the files identified in the **SELECT** statements above—in this program, CARD-FILE and PRINT-FILE.

Invoice Register

Invoice Number	Branch Number	Salesperson Number	Customer Number	Item Number	Description	Qnty	Unit Price	Sales Amount
8101	01	19	71002	135	grph paper	16	$3.10	$49.60
8101	01	19	71002	216	mrkng pen	45	$1.40	$63.00
8101	01	19	71002	263	typwrtr rbn	300	$2.88	$864.00
			INVOICE TOTAL = $976.60					
8102	01	34	69005	015	paper clips	7	$ .93	$6.51
8102	01	34	69005	032	correx fluid	16	$1.60	$25.60
			INVOICE TOTAL = $32.11					
8103	03	42	70013	359	large clips	88	$ .82	$72.16
8103	03	42	70013	383	record bks	9	$8.10	$72.90
8103	03	42	70013	424	ntbks, xl	30	$3.50	$105.00
8103	03	42	70013	537	ntbks, sm	15	$ .94	$14.10
			INVOICE TOTAL = $264.16					
8104	03	51	73121	024	lrg eraser	80	$ .50	$40.00
8104	03	51	73121	408	pencils, bx	30	$1.45	$43.50
			INVOICE TOTAL = $83.50					
8105	03	52	68055	056	clip board	60	$5.60	$336.60
			INVOICE TOTAL = $336.00					
8106	03	56	73115	257	tape, roll	176	$ .83	$146.08
8106	03	56	73115	312	dsk orgnzr	20	$3.10	$62.00
8106	03	56	73115	560	tacks, bx	97	$ .55	$53.35
8106	03	56	73115	632	folders	130	$ .60	$78.00
			INVOICE TOTAL = $339.43					

TOTAL RECORDS PROCESSED = 16   FINAL TOTAL = $2,031.80

Figure B.1: Table Produced by COBOL Invoice Program

```
        IDENTIFICATION DIVISION.
        PROGRAM-ID.
                INVOICES.
        AUTHOR.
                D HERGERT.
        REMARKS.
                THIS PROGRAM CALCULATES INVOICE TOTALS, AND
                PRODUCES AN INVOICE REPORT.


        ENVIRONMENT DIVISION.
        CONFIGURATION SECTION.
        SOURCE-COMPUTER.
                IBM-370.
        OBJECT-COMPUTER.
                IBM-370.
        SPECIAL-NAMES.
                C01 IS TOP-OF-PAGE.

        INPUT-OUTPUT SECTION.

        FILE-CONTROL.

                SELECT CARD-FILE
                    ASSIGN TO UR-S-SYSIN.
                SELECT PRINT-FILE
                    ASSIGN TO UR-S-SYSPRINT.

        DATA DIVISION.
        FILE SECTION.

        FD  CARD-FILE
            RECORDING MODE IS F
            LABEL RECORDS ARE OMITTED
            RECORD CONTAINS 80 CHARACTERS
            DATA RECORD IS INVOICE-CARD.

        01  INVOICE-CARD.
            05  FILLER              PIC X(06).
            05  INVOICE-NO          PIC 9(04).
            05  BRANCH-NO           PIC X(02).
            05  SALESPERSON-NO      PIC X(02).
            05  FILLER              PIC X(03).
            05  CUSTOMER-NO         PIC X(05).
            05  QUANTITY-SOLD       PIC 9(04).
            05  DESCRIPTION         PIC X(15).
            05  FILLER              PIC X(17).
            05  ITEM-NO             PIC X(03).
            05  UNIT-PRICE          PIC 9V99.
            05  FILLER              PIC X(16).
```

Figure B.2: COBOL "Invoices" Program

```
FD  PRINT-FILE
    RECORDING MODE IS F
    LABEL RECORDS ARE OMITTED
    RECORD CONTAINS 121 CHARACTERS
    DATA RECORD IS PRINT-REC.

01  PRINT-REC.
    05  FILLER              PIC X(01).
    05  PRINT-LINE          PIC X(120).

WORKING-STORAGE SECTION.

77  WS-PREVIOUS-INVOICE     PIC 9(04)      VALUE ZEROS.
77  WS-AMT-OF-SALE          PIC 999V99.
77  WS-AMT-OF-INVOICE       PIC 999V99.
77  WS-AMT-OF-TOTAL         PIC 9999V99    VALUE ZEROS.
77  WS-RECORDS-PROCESSED    PIC 999        VALUE ZEROS.
77  WS-END-OF-FILE          PIC XXX        VALUE SPACES.
77  WS-END-INV-PERFORM      PIC XXX        VALUE SPACES.

01  WS-DETAIL-LINE                         VALUE SPACES.
    05  FILLER              PIC X(18).
    05  INVOICE-NO          PIC 9(04).
    05  FILLER              PIC X(06).
    05  BRANCH-NO           PIC X(02).
    05  FILLER              PIC X(08).
    05  SALESPERSON-NO      PIC X(02).
    05  FILLER              PIC X(08).
    05  CUSTOMER-NO         PIC X(05).
    05  FILLER              PIC X(06).
    05  ITEM-NO             PIC X(03).
    05  FILLER              PIC X(04).
    05  DESCRIPTION         PIC X(15).
    05  FILLER              PIC X(03).
    05  QUANTITY-SOLD       PIC ZZZ9.
    05  FILLER              PIC X(02).
    05  UNIT-PRICE          PIC $$.99.
    05  FILLER              PIC X(02).
    05  SALES-AMOUNT        PIC $$$,$$$.99.
    05  FILLER              PIC X(13).

01  WS-TITLE-LINE.
    05  FILLER              PIC X(51)      VALUE SPACES.
    05  FILLER              PIC X(16)      VALUE
                                           'INVOICE REGISTER'.
    05  FILLER              PIC X(53)      VALUE SPACES.

01  WS-HEADING-LINE-ONE.
    05  FILLER              PIC X(17)      VALUE SPACES.
    05  FILLER              PIC X(17)      VALUE
                                           'INVOICE  BRANCH  '.
    05  FILLER              PIC X(13)      VALUE
                                           'SALESPERSON  '.
```

Figure B.2: COBOL "Invoices" Program (cont.)

```
       05  FILLER              PIC X(19)      VALUE
                                              'CUSTOMER      ITEM   '.
       05  FILLER              PIC X(18)      VALUE
                                              'DESCRIPTION         '.
       05  FILLER              PIC X(20)      VALUE
                                              'QNTY  UNIT      SALES'.
       05  FILLER              PIC X(16)      VALUE SPACES.

   01  WS-HEADING-LINE-TWO.
       05  FILLER              PIC X(17)      VALUE SPACES.
       05  FILLER              PIC X(47)      VALUE
               'NUMBER   NUMBER    NUMBER      NUMBER     NUMBER'.
       05  FILLER              PIC X(26)      VALUE SPACES.
       05  FILLER              PIC X(15)      VALUE
                                              'PRICE     AMOUNT'.
       05  FILLER              PIC X(15)      VALUE SPACES.

   01  WS-INVOICE-TOTAL-LINE.
       05  FILLER              PIC X(59)      VALUE SPACES.
       05  FILLER              PIC X(16)      VALUE
                                              'INVOICE TOTAL = '.
       05  TOTAL-ONE           PIC $$$$.99.
       05  FILLER              PIC X(38)      VALUE SPACES.

   01  WS-FINAL-TOTAL-LINE.
       05  FILLER              PIC X(20)      VALUE SPACES.
       05  FILLER              PIC X(26)      VALUE
                                       'TOTAL RECORDS PROCESSED = '.
       05  RECORDS-PROC-TOT    PIC ZZ9.
       05  FILLER              PIC X(10)      VALUE SPACES.
       05  FILLER              PIC X(14)      VALUE
                                              'FINAL TOTAL = '.
       05  TOTAL-TWO           PIC $$,$$$.99.
       05  FILLER              PIC X(38)      VALUE SPACES.


PROCEDURE DIVISION.

    PERFORM 100-HOUSEKEEPING.
    PERFORM 200-INVOICE-TOTALING
        UNTIL WS-END-INV-PERFORM = 'YES'.
    PERFORM 400-FINAL-RECORDING.
    CLOSE CARD-FILE, PRINT-FILE.
    STOP RUN.

100-HOUSEKEEPING SECTION.

    OPEN INPUT CARD-FILE, OUTPUT PRINT-FILE.
    READ CARD-FILE, AT END MOVE 'YES' TO WS-END-OF-FILE.

    MOVE SPACES TO PRINT-REC.
    MOVE WS-TITLE-LINE TO PRINT-LINE.
    WRITE PRINT-REC AFTER ADVANCING TOP-OF-PAGE LINES.
```

Figure B.2: COBOL "Invoices" Program (cont.)

```
      MOVE SPACES TO PRINT-REC.
      MOVE WS-HEADING-LINE-ONE TO PRINT-LINE.
      WRITE PRINT-REC AFTER ADVANCING 3 LINES.

      MOVE SPACES TO PRINT-REC.
      MOVE WS-HEADING-LINE-TWO TO PRINT-LINE.
      WRITE PRINT-REC AFTER ADVANCING 1 LINES.

      MOVE SPACES TO PRINT-REC.
      WRITE PRINT-REC AFTER ADVANCING 2 LINES.


200-INVOICE-TOTALING SECTION.

      MOVE ZEROS TO WS-AMT-OF-INVOICE.
      MOVE INVOICE-NO OF INVOICE-CARD TO WS-PREVIOUS-INVOICE.
      PERFORM 300-SALES-TOTALING
          UNTIL WS-END-OF-FILE = 'YES'
          OR INVOICE-NO OF INVOICE-CARD
          IS NOT EQUAL TO WS-PREVIOUS-INVOICE.

      ADD WS-AMT-OF-INVOICE TO WS-AMT-OF-TOTAL.

      MOVE SPACES TO PRINT-REC.
      MOVE WS-AMT-OF-INVOICE TO TOTAL-ONE.
      MOVE WS-INVOICE-TOTAL-LINE TO PRINT-LINE.
      WRITE PRINT-REC AFTER ADVANCING 2 LINES.

      MOVE SPACES TO PRINT-REC.
      WRITE PRINT-REC AFTER ADVANCING 2 LINES.

      IF WS-END-OF-FILE = 'YES'
          MOVE 'YES' TO WS-END-INV-PERFORM.

300-SALES-TOTALING SECTION.

      MOVE ZEROS TO WS-AMT-OF-SALE.
      COMPUTE WS-AMT-OF-SALE ROUNDED
      = QUANTITY-SOLD OF INVOICE-CARD * UNIT-PRICE OF INVOICE-CARD.
      ADD WS-AMT-OF-SALE TO WS-AMT-OF-INVOICE.
      MOVE WS-AMT-OF-SALE TO SALES-AMOUNT.
      MOVE CORRESPONDING INVOICE-CARD TO WS-DETAIL-LINE.

      MOVE SPACES TO PRINT-REC.
      MOVE WS-DETAIL-LINE TO PRINT-LINE.
      WRITE PRINT-REC AFTER ADVANCING 1 LINES.

      ADD 1 TO WS-RECORDS-PROCESSED.
      READ CARD-FILE, AT END MOVE 'YES' TO WS-END-OF-FILE.
```

Figure B.2: COBOL "Invoices" Program (cont.)

```
400-FINAL-RECORDING SECTION.

    MOVE WS-RECORDS-PROCESSED TO RECORDS-PROC-TOT.
    MOVE WS-AMT-OF-TOTAL TO TOTAL-TWO.
    MOVE SPACES TO PRINT-REC.
    MOVE WS-FINAL-TOTAL-LINE TO PRINT-LINE.
    WRITE PRINT-REC AFTER ADVANCING 2 LINES.
```

Figure B.2: COBOL "Invoices" Program (cont.)

Let us briefly examine the description of the CARD-FILE. The first two clauses of the **FD** statement are characteristic of data card records:

RECORDING MODE IS F

LABEL RECORDS ARE OMITTED

The F stands for fixed-length records (as opposed to V, variable-length records); label records are used for other recording media, such as tapes and disks. The next clause defines the length of the record:

RECORD CONTAINS 80 **CHARACTERS**

Finally, the last clause in the **FD** statement identifies the data structure into which information from the cards will be read:

DATA RECORD IS INVOICE-CARD.

The INVOICE-CARD record is described next; it contains a dozen field descriptions, or "elementary items," which, in total, define how the 80 columns of the data card will be read and interpreted. Each elementary item has a picture clause (**PIC**). This clause tells what *type* of data (numeric, alphabetic, alphanumeric) will be read into each field, and how many characters or digits each field will contain. An X in the **PIC** clause stands for alphanumeric data; a 9 means numeric data. The table in Figure B.3 is an interpretation of the INVOICE-CARD in terms of the 80 columns of the data card.

Notice that numbers that will not be used in calculations may be defined as alphanumeric.

The numeric field UNIT-PRICE requires a special PIC clause:

05   UNIT-PRICE   **PIC** 9V99

The V represents an "assumed" decimal point. This decimal point is not punched into the data card; however, when the three digits are read for UNIT-PRICE, the decimal point will be recorded after the first digit.

The output record PRINT-REC is 121 characters long. The first character of each line is reserved for carriage control, leaving 120 characters for the actual PRINT-LINE. This PRINT-LINE will receive several different data records; six records in the **WORKING-STORAGE SECTION** define the different formats of the output print line: a main "detail" line contains the invoice information for each sale; in addition, a title line, two heading lines, and two total lines are defined. The **VALUE** clause, after the **PIC** clause, initializes data items to a given value.

The **WORKING-STORAGE SECTION** also contains *77-level* data items; these are intermediate data items that will be used as "variables" in the calculations of the **PROCEDURE DIVISION**.

Finally, notice that several of the **PIC** clauses in the **WORKING-STORAGE SECTION** illustrate COBOL's editing characters. A "floating" dollar sign with commas is represented as:

    PIC $$$,$$$.99

The editing character Z suppresses initial zeros:

    PIC ZZZ9

Column Numbers	Description
1 - 6	blank
7 - 10	invoice number (numeric)
11 - 12	branch number (alphanumeric)
13 - 14	salesperson number (alphanumeric)
15 - 17	blank
18 - 22	customer number (alphanumeric)
23 - 26	quantity sold (numeric)
27 - 41	description of item (alphanumeric)
42 - 58	blank
59 - 61	item number (alphanumeric)
62 - 64	unit price (numeric)
65 - 80	blank

Figure B.3: The INVOICE-CARD

The **PROCEDURE DIVISION** expresses the logic of the program. In the Invoices program, the first five statements of the **PROCEDURE DIVISION** constitute the main block of the program; three **PERFORM** statements in this block control the execution of the blocks below.

The HOUSEKEEPING **SECTION** is performed first. This section opens the input and output files, reads the first input record, and prints the title and headings of the report. Notice the sequence of statements for printing a line:

> **MOVE SPACES TO** PRINT-REC.
>
> **MOVE** WS-TITLE-LINE **TO** PRINT-LINE.
>
> **MOVE** PRINT-REC **AFTER ADVANCING TOP-OF-PAGE LINES**.

The first statement clears the PRINT-REC of previous data or "garbage". The second statement moves the appropriate record to the 120-character PRINT-LINE. The third statement writes the line, with the **AFTER ADVANCING** clause to determine spacing.

The INVOICE-TOTALING **SECTION** is executed within a loop until WS-END-INV-PERFORM is switched to 'YES':

> **PERFORM** 200-INVOICE-TOTALING
>
> **UNTIL** WS-END-INV-PERFORM = 'YES'.

This section initializes the total invoice amount (WS-AMT-OF-INVOICE) to zero and keeps a record of the invoice number (in WS-PREVIOUS-INVOICE) in order to check for a new invoice number:

> **MOVE** INVOICE-NO **OF** INVOICE-CARD **TO** WS-PREVIOUS-INVOICE.

The SALES-TOTALING **SECTION**, which contains the **COMPUTE** statement to find the amount of each sale, is also executed within a loop:

> **PERFORM** 300-SALES-TOTALING
>
> **UNTIL** WS-END-OF-FILE = 'YES'
>
> **OR** INVOICE-NO **OF** INVOICE-CARD
>
> **IS NOT EQUAL TO** WS-PREVIOUS-INVOICE.

This loop-within-a-loop performs the following sequence of events:

1. A sales line is printed, along with the total amount of the sale (SALES-TOTALING).

2. A new input record is read (SALES-TOTALING).

3. If the invoice number is different from the previous invoice number, then a total for the previous invoice is printed (INVOICE-TOTALING), and WS-AMT-OF-INVOICE is reinitialized to zero for the accumulation of the next invoice total.

4. The sequence of events repeats from step 1; the looping stops when the end of the input file is reached.

When all of the records have been processed, the FINAL-RECORDING **SECTION** prints the total line for all the invoices. The main procedure block ends execution of the program with the following statements:

CLOSE CARD-FILE, PRINT-FILE.
STOP RUN.

Pascal

This interactive Pascal program is patterned after the monthly sales report program of Chapter 3. The main difference between the two programs is that the Pascal program stores the monthly sales data in an array and produces a graph after all the data have been input. Figure B.4 shows an example of the output from this program (the input dialogue is not shown).

The listing for this program appears in Figure B.5. The main program, which calls the procedures above it, is located at the very end of the listing. Notice that the comment delimiters (∗ and ∗) are used to mark off sections of this program or to identify interesting features.

The main program first calls procedure INSTRUCTIONS to write a description of the program, then procedure GETDATA for the required input values. A **REPEAT/UNTIL** loop then calls PRINTGRAPH to produce as many versions of the graph as the user wants to see; for each iteration of the loop, the user can choose a new scale factor for the graph.

Procedure PRINTGRAPH contains the following loop to print the "bars" of the graph:

```
FOR J := 1 TO UNITSSOLD[I] DIV FACTOR DO
    WRITE(GRAPHCHR);
```

```
           UNIT SALES FOR 5-MONTH PERIOD
           BEGINNING SEP 81
           (ONE '*' = 5 UNITS)

           SEP 81  ==>   * * * * * * * * *

           OCT 81  ==>   * * * * * * * * * *

           NOV 81  ==>   * * * * * * * * * * * * *

           DEC 81  ==>   * * * * * * * * * * * * * *

           JAN 82  ==>   * * * * * * * * * * * * * * * *

           TOTAL UNITS SOLD DURING PERIOD = 373.00
           AVERAGE MONTHLY SALES IN UNITS = 75
```

Figure B.4: Monthly Sales Report Output (Pascal)

```
   (*
    *    PROGRAM SALES PRODUCES A BAR GRAPH
    *    OF MONTHLY UNIT SALES FOR A SPECIFIED
    *    PERIOD; IT ALSO COMPUTES THE AVERAGE
    *    MONTHLY UNIT SALES FOR THE PERIOD.
    *)

   PROGRAM SALES;

   CONST
     MONTHMAX = 60;    (* MAXIMUM NUMBER OF MONTHS
                          THE PROGRAM CAN HANDLE    *)
     GRAPHCHR = '*';   (* CHARACTER USED TO PRODUCE
                          BAR GRAPH                 *)

   TYPE
     MONTHRANGE = 1..MONTHMAX;
     MONTHTYPE  = ARRAY[MONTHRANGE] OF INTEGER;

   VAR
     MONTHNAME : STRING;
     MONTH,
     YEAR,
     NUMMONTHS,
     SCALEFAC,
```

Figure B.5: Pascal Program SALES

```
    AVERAGEUNITS : INTEGER;
    TOTALUNITS   : REAL;
    UNITSSOLD    : MONTHTYPE;  (* ARRAY OF UNITS SOLD PER MONTH *)
    ANSWER       : CHAR;

PROCEDURE INSTRUCTIONS;
  BEGIN
     WRITELN;
     WRITELN ('MONTHLY SALES PROGRAM');
     WRITELN ('----------------------');
     WRITELN;
     WRITELN ('THIS PROGRAM PRODUCES STATISTICS');
     WRITELN ('AND A GRAPH OF MONTHLY SALES FOR');
     WRITELN ('A SPECIFIED PERIOD.');
     WRITELN ('INPUT REQUIRED:');
     WRITELN ('      * NUMBER OF MONTHS IN PERIOD');
     WRITELN ('      * BEGINNING MONTH/YEAR OF PERIOD');
     WRITELN ('      * UNIT SALES FOR EACH MONTH OF PERIOD');
     WRITELN ('      * SCALE FACTOR FOR GRAPH');
     WRITELN;
     WRITELN;
  END;


(*
 *   PROCEDURE CHOOSEMONTH SUPPLIES ABBREVIATED NAMES
 *   FOR EACH OF THE TWELVE MONTHS.  AN INTEGER
 *   FROM 1 TO 12 IS PASSED TO THE FORMAL VALUE
 *   PARAMETER M, AND THE NAME OF THE MONTH IS RETURNED
 *   VIA THE VARIABLE PARAMETER NAME.
 *)

PROCEDURE CHOOSEMONTH (M: INTEGER;
               VAR  NAME: STRING);

VAR
   TEMP : STRING;

BEGIN
   CASE M OF
    1  :   TEMP := 'JAN';
    2  :   TEMP := 'FEB';
    3  :   TEMP := 'MAR';
    4  :   TEMP := 'APR';
    5  :   TEMP := 'MAY';
    6  :   TEMP := 'JUN';
    7  :   TEMP := 'JUL';
    8  :   TEMP := 'AUG';
    9  :   TEMP := 'SEP';
   10  :   TEMP := 'OCT';
   11  :   TEMP := 'NOV';
   12  :   TEMP := 'DEC';
   END;
   NAME := TEMP;
END;
```

Figure B.5: Pascal Program SALES (cont.)

```
PROCEDURE GETDATA;
VAR
  TEMPMONTH,
  TEMPYEAR,
  I          : INTEGER;

BEGIN
  REPEAT
    BEGIN
      WRITELN('NUMBER OF MONTHS (1 TO ', MONTHMAX, ')? ');
      READ(NUMMONTHS);
    END
  UNTIL (NUMMONTHS > 1) AND (NUMMONTHS <= MONTHMAX);
  WRITELN ('BEGINNING MONTH AND YEAR');

  REPEAT
    BEGIN
      WRITE('MM<1..12>? ');
      READLN(MONTH);
      WRITE('YY<1..99>? ');
      READLN(YEAR);
    END
  UNTIL (MONTH >= 1) AND (MONTH <= 12) AND
        (YEAR  >= 1) AND (YEAR  <= 99);

  TEMPMONTH := MONTH;
  TEMPYEAR := YEAR;
  TOTALUNITS := 0;

  FOR I := 1 TO NUMMONTHS DO
    BEGIN
      WRITE('UNITS SOLD IN ');
      CHOOSEMONTH(TEMPMONTH, MONTHNAME);
      WRITE(MONTHNAME, ' ', TEMPYEAR, '? ');
      READLN(UNITSSOLD[I]);
      TOTALUNITS := TOTALUNITS + UNITSSOLD[I];
      TEMPMONTH := TEMPMONTH + 1;
      IF TEMPMONTH > 12 THEN
        BEGIN
          TEMPMONTH := 1;
          TEMPYEAR  := TEMPYEAR + 1
        END
    END
END;

(*
 *  PROCEDURE PRINTGRAPH PRODUCES THE GRAPH,
 *  PROPORTIONED BY THE VALUE OF FACTOR.
 *)
```

Figure B.5: Pascal Program SALES (cont.)

```
PROCEDURE PRINTGRAPH (FACTOR : INTEGER);
  VAR
    TEMPMONTH,
    TEMPYEAR,
    I,
    J            : INTEGER;


BEGIN
  WRITELN('UNIT SALES FOR ', NUMMONTHS, '-MONTH PERIOD');
  CHOOSEMONTH(MONTH, MONTHNAME);
  WRITELN('BEGINNING ', MONTHNAME, ' ', YEAR);
  WRITELN('(ONE  ''', GRAPHCHR, ''' = ', FACTOR, ' UNITS)');


  WRITELN;
  TEMPMONTH := MONTH;
  TEMPYEAR  := YEAR;
  FOR I := 1 TO NUMMONTHS DO
    BEGIN
      WRITE(MONTHNAME, ' ', TEMPYEAR, ' ==> ');

      (*
       *   THIS LOOP PRINTS EACH 'BAR' OF THE GRAPH
       *)

      FOR J := 1 TO UNITSSOLD[I] DIV FACTOR DO
        WRITE(GRAPHCHR);
      WRITELN;
      TEMPMONTH := TEMPMONTH + 1;
      IF TEMPMONTH > 12 THEN


        BEGIN
          TEMPMONTH := 1;
          TEMPYEAR := TEMPYEAR + 1
        END;
      CHOOSEMONTH(TEMPMONTH, MONTHNAME);
    END
END;


BEGIN (* MAIN PROGRAM *)
  INSTRUCTIONS;
  GETDATA;
  WRITELN;
  REPEAT
    WRITELN('ONE GRAPHICS CHARACTER (''', GRAPHCHR, ''') ');
    WRITE('REPRESENTS HOW MANY UNITS SOLD? ');
    READLN(SCALEFAC);
```

Figure B.5: Pascal Program SALES (cont.)

```
      WRITELN;
      WRITELN;
      WRITELN;
      WRITELN('--------------------------------------------');
      PRINTGRAPH(SCALEFAC);
      WRITELN;
      WRITELN('TOTAL UNITS SOLD DURING PERIOD = ', TOTALUNITS:8:2);
      WRITELN('AVERAGE MONTHLY SALES IN UNITS = ',
              ROUND(TOTALUNITS/NUMMONTHS));
      WRITELN;
      WRITELN('--------------------------------------------');
      WRITELN;
      WRITE('ANOTHER SCALE FACTOR? <Y> OR <N> ');
      READLN(ANSWER);
    UNTIL ANSWER = 'N';
  END.   (* MAIN PROGRAM *)
```

Figure B.5: Pascal Program SALES (cont.)

GRAPHCHR is a constant, defined at the beginning of the program. The **DIV** operation produces a truncated quotient. The length of each bar of the graph is thus determined by the number of units sold during the appropriate month, divided by the scale factor for the graph.

Finally, notice that procedure CHOOSEMONTH is used both by GETDATA and PRINTGRAPH to determine the names of the months. The main feature of CHOOSEMONTH is a **CASE** statement that sets the string TEMP to the correct month name corresponding to the value of the integer M. CHOOSEMONTH returns the string to the calling program in the variable parameter NAME.

FORTRAN

Program TAXEFF is a FORTRAN version of the depreciation program described in Chapter 4. It produces the same three tables: the present value of the tax savings under three depreciation methods—straight line, sum-of-the-years' digits, and double-declining-balance. The three subroutines of this FORTRAN program—DDB, DISCNT, and SYD—can be compared almost line-by-line with the corresponding BASIC subroutines listed in Chapter 4.

TAXEFF begins by reading a data card that contains the four input values. These values are "echoed" at the beginning of the output report, before the three tables are produced. Thus, the user has a printed record of the input values for any given run of the program. The record might look something like this:

AFTER — TAX EFFECTS OF DEPRECIATION

ORIGINAL COST OF EQUIPMENT = $ 50000.00
EXPECTED USEFUL LIFE OF EQUIPMENT = 12 YEARS
INCOME TAX RATE = 35.0 PERCENT
DESIRED RATE OF RETURN ON INVESTMENT AFTER TAXES = 18.0 PERCENT

The listing of the FORTRAN program appears in Figure B.6. The program is documented by abundant comment lines (indicated by a C in column 1).

```
      PROGRAM TAXEFF
C                    THIS PROGRAM COMPUTES THE EFFECT OF
C                    DEPRECIATION ON INCOME TAXES IN PRESENT
C                    VALUE TERMS.  IT CARRIES OUT ITS
C                    CALCULATIONS USING THREE COMMON DEPRECIATION
C                    METHODS--STRAIGHT LINE, SUM-OF-THE-YEARS'-
C                    DIGITS, AND DOUBLE-DECLINING-BALANCE.
C
C                    THE PROGRAM WILL HANDLE A MAXIMUM OF 30
C                    YEARS USEFUL LIFE.
C
      DIMENSION XMULT(30), DISFAC(30), DDBDEP(30)
C
C                    READ THE DATA CARD.
C
      READ (5,100) COST, NYEARS, TXRATE, ERATE
  100 FORMAT (F10.2, I2, 2F3.1)
C
C                    WRITE ERROR MESSAGE IF NYEARS > 30.
C
      IF (NYEARS .LE. 30) GO TO 10
      WRITE (6,110) NYEARS
  110 FORMAT (1H1, 8HYEARS = , I2 / 1H0, 'PROGRAM ONLY HANDLES
     +UP TO 30-YEAR USEFUL LIFE')
      STOP
C
C                    SUBROUTINE DISCNT COMPUTES DISCOUNT FACTORS
C
   10 CALL DISCNT (NYEARS, ERATE, DISFAC, ANFAC)
C
```

Figure B.6: FORTRAN TAXEFF Program

```
C                        ECHO THE INPUT DATA
C
      WRITE (6,120) COST, NYEARS, TXRATE, ERATE
 120  FORMAT (1H1 /// 42X, 'AFTER-TAX EFFECTS OF DEPRECIATION'
     +/// '0', 'ORIGINAL COST OF EQUIPMENT = $', F11.2, / ' ',
     +'EXPECTED USEFUL LIFE OF EQUIPMENT =  ', I2, ' YEARS' /
     +' ', 'INCOME TAX RATE  = ', F4.1, ' PERCENT' / ' ',
     +'DESIRED RATE OF RETURN ON INVESTMENT AFTER TAXES = ',
     +F4.1, ' PERCENT' ///// 45X, 'STRAIGHT-LINE DEPRECIATION'
     +///)
C
C                 PRINT TITLE AND HEADINGS FOR FIRST PAGE.
C
      WRITE (6,130) TXRATE, TXRATE
 130  FORMAT (' ', 25X, 'TOTAL SAVINGS IN', 9X, 'YEARLY SAVINGS
     + IN', 8X, 'DISCOUNT FACTOR--' / ' ', 26X, 'INCOME TAX AT',
     +13X, 'INCOME TAX AT', 12X, 'PRESENT VALUE', 17X, 'TOTAL'/
     +' ', 'ANNUAL DEPRECIATION', 8X, F4.1, ' PERCENT', 14X, F4.1,
     +' PERCENT', 11X, 'OF ANNUITY', 15X, 'PRESENT VALUE'///)
C
C                      THIS SECTION COMPUTES THE PRESENT VALUE
C                      FOR STRAIGHT-LINE DEPRECIATION.
C
      XNYEAR = NYEARS
      SLD1 = COST / XNYEAR
      SLD2 = (TXRATE / 100.0) * COST
      SLD3 = SLD2 / XNYEAR
      SLD4 = SLD3 * ANFAC
      WRITE (6, 140) SLD1, SLD2, SLD3, ANFAC, SLD4
 140  FORMAT (' ', 3X, 1H$, F11.2, 12X, 1H$, F11.2, 12X, 1H$,
     +F11.2, 17X, F7.4, 17X, 1H$, F11.2)
C
C                      THIS SECTION COMPUTES THE PRESENT VALUE
C                      FOR THE SYD METHOD. SUBROUTINE SYD
C                      COMPUTES THE SYD MULTIPLIERS.
C
      CALL SYD (NYEARS, TXRATE)
      WRITE (6, 200)
 200  FORMAT ('1' /// ' ', 40X, 'SUM-OF-THE-YEARS-DIGITS DEPRECI
     +ATION' ///)
      WRITE (6, 210) TXRATE
 210  FORMAT (' ', 28X, 'INCOME TAX SAVINGS', / ' ', ' YEAR', 7X,
     +'DEPRECIATION', 5X, 'AT ', F4.1, ' PERCENT', 10X, 'PRESENT
     + VALUE DISCOUNT FACTOR', 6X, 'PRESENT VALUE', 4X, 'TOTAL P
     +RESENT VALUE' ///)
      TOTSYD = 0.0
      DO 20 ISYD = 1, NYEARS
      SYD1 = COST * XMULT(ISYD)
      SYD2 = SYD1 * (TXRATE / 100.0)
      SYD3 = SYD2 * DISFAC(ISYD)
      TOTSYD = TOTSYD + SYD3
```

Figure B.6: FORTRAN TAXEFF Program (cont.)

```
        WRITE (6,220) ISYD, SYD1, SYD2, DISFAC(ISYD), SYD3
 220    FORMAT ('0', 2X, I2, 4X, 1H$, F11.2, 8X, 1H$, F11.2, 24X,
       +F6.5, 19X, 1H$, F11.2)
  20    CONTINUE
        WRITE (6, 230) TOTSYD
 230    FORMAT ('0' / 119X, 1H$, F11.2)
C
C                       THIS SECTION COMPUTES THE DDB METHOD PRESENT
C                       VALUES.  SUBROUTINE DDB COMPUTES THE DEPRE-
C                       CIATION FIGURES FOR THIS METHOD.
C
        CALL DDB (COST, NYEARS, DDBDEP)
        WRITE (6, 300)
 300    FORMAT ('1' /// ' ', 40X, 'DOUBLE-DECLINING-BALANCE DEPRECI
       +ATION' ///)
        WRITE (6, 210) TXRATE
        TOTDDB = 0.0
        DO 30 IDDB = 1, NYEARS
        DDB1 = DDBDEP(IDDB) * (TXRATE / 100.0)
        DDB2 = DDB1 * DISFAC(IDDB)
        TOTDDB = TOTDDB + DDB2
        WRITE (6, 220) IDDB, DDBDEP(IDDB), DDB1, DISFAC(IDDB), DDB2
  30    CONTINUE
        WRITE (6, 310) TOTDDB
 310    FORMAT ('0' / 109X, 1H$, F11.2 / '1')
        STOP
        END
C
C
C                       SUBROUTINE DDB.
C                       COMPUTES THE YEARLY DEPRECIATION VALUES
C                       FOR THE DOUBLE-DECLINING-BALANCE METHOD
C                       AND STORES THESE VALUES IN THE ARRAY
C                       DDBDEP.
C
        SUBROUTINE DDB (COST, NYEARS, DDBDEP)
        DIMENSION DDBDEP(30)
        XNYEAR = NYEARS
        DDBDEP(1) = (COST / XNYEAR) * 2.0
        TOTDEP = DDBDEP(1)
        N1 = NYEARS - 1
        DO 10 I = 2, N1
        DDBDEP(I) = ((COST - TOTDEP) / XNYEAR) * 2.0
        TOTDEP = TOTDEP + DDBDEP (I)
  10    CONTINUE
        DDBDEP(NYEARS) = COST - TOTDEP
        RETURN
        END
```

Figure B.6: FORTRAN TAXEFF Program (cont.)

```
C
C
C                      SUBROUTINE DISCNT.
C                      RECEIVES THE NUMBER OF YEARS OF USEFUL
C                      LIFE OF THE ITEM TO BE DEPRECIATED, AND
C                      THE EXPECTED RATE OF RETURN ON INVESTEMENT.
C                      COMPUTES THE YEARLY DISCOUNT FACTOR AND THE
C                      ANNUITY FACTOR.
C
        SUBROUTINE DISCNT (NYEARS, ERATE, DISFAC, ANFAC)
        DIMENSION DISFAC(30)
        ANFAC = 0.0
        DO 10 K = 1, NYEARS
        DISFAC(K) = 1.0 / ((1.0 + (ERATE / 100.0)) ** K)
        ANFAC = ANFAC + DISFAC(K)
    10  CONTINUE
        RETURN
        END
C
C
C                      SUBROUTINE SYD.
C                      RECEIVES THE NUMBER OF YEARS OF USEFUL LIFE
C                      AND COMPUTES EACH YEARLY MULTIPLIER FOR
C                      SUM-OF-THE-YEARS'-DIGITS DEPRECIATION.
C                      STORES THESE VALUE IN THE ARRAY XMULT.
C
        SUBROUTINE SYD (NYEARS, XMULT)
        DIMENSION XMULT(30)
        INTEGER DENOM
        DENOM = 0
        DO 10 M = 1, NYEARS
        DENOM = DENOM + M
    10  CONTINUE
        XNYEAR = NYEARS
        XDENOM = DENOM
        DO 20 I = 1, NYEARS
        XI = I - 1
        XMULT(I) = (XNYEAR - XI) / XDENOM
    20  CONTINUE
        RETURN
        END
```

Figure B.6: FORTRAN TAXEFF Program (cont.)

Much of the bulk of this program is taken up by FORMAT statements that describe the output lines. The table in Figure B.7 explains the symbols used in these **FORMAT** statements. Notice that a literal string can be represented in two ways—either within quotes:

'YEARS = ',

or as a Hollerith field:

    8HYEARS = ,

The integer before the H indicates how many characters after the H belong to the Hollerith field.

Finally, since "mixed-mode" arithmetic (reals and integers mixed in the same arithmetic statement) can produce unexpected results in FORTRAN, type conversions are effected by assignment statements to avoid mixed mode. For example, the statement:

    XNYEAR = NYEARS

assigns the value of the integer NYEARS to the real variable XNYEAR before the statement:

    SLD1 = COST/XNYEAR

Symbol	Example	Explanation of Example
F	F10.2	10-character "floating-point" number; 2 digits after the decimal point.
I	I2	2-digit integer.
X	26X	26 spaces.
/	////	4 carriage returns
+	+IN'	Continuation of FORMAT statement; the + appears in column 6.
	Carriage Control Characters	
1	'1' or 1H1	New page.
0	'0' or 1H0	Double spacing.
blank	' ' or 1H	Single spacing.

Figure B.7: FORTRAN FORMAT Symbols

Recall that variable names beginning with the letters I, J, K, L, M, and N represent integer types, and variable names with other initial letters represent real, or "floating-point" types. These specifications may be changed by REAL or INTEGER statements, as in subroutine SYD:

INTEGER DENOM

This statement defines DENOM to be of type INTEGER.

Bibliography

Dopuch, Nicholas, and Birnberg, Jacob G. *Cost Accounting: Accounting Data for Management's Decisions*. New York: Harcourt, Brace & World, 1969.

Gottfried, Byron S. *Programming with BASIC*. New York: McGraw-Hill, 1975.

Grauer, Robert T., and Crawford, Marshal A. *COBOL: A Pragmatic Approach*. Englewood Cliffs, N.J.: Prentice-Hall, 1978.

Grogono, Peter. *Programming in Pascal*. rev. ed. Reading, Mass.: Addison-Wesley, 1980.

Horngren, Charles T. *Introduction to Management Accounting*. 3rd ed. Englewood Cliffs, N.J.: Prentice-Hall, 1978.

Khailany, Asad. *Business Programming in FORTRAN IV and ANSI FORTRAN 77: A Structured Approach*. Englewood Cliffs, N.J.: Prentice-Hall, 1981.

Lien, David A. *The BASIC Handbook: Encyclopedia of the BASIC Computer Language*. 2nd ed. San Diego, Calif.: Compusoft Publishing, 1981.

Mateosian, Richard. *Inside BASIC Games*. Berkeley: Sybex, 1981.

McCracken, Daniel D. *A Guide to Fortran IV Programming*. New York: John Wiley & Sons, 1972.

———. *A Simplified Guide to Fortran Programming*. New York: John Wiley & Sons, 1974.

Miller, Alan R. *Pascal Programs for Scientists and Engineers*. Berkeley: Sybex, 1981.

———. *BASIC Programs for Scientists and Engineers*. Berkeley: Sybex, 1982.

Ralston, Anthony, ed. *Encyclopedia of Computer Science.* New York: Van Nostrand Reinhold Company, 1976.

Spirer, Herbert F. *Business Statistics: A Problem-Solving Approach.* Homewood, Illinois: Richard D. Irwin, 1975.

Welsch, Glenn A., and Anthony, Robert N. *Fundamentals of Financial Accounting.* rev. ed. Homewood, Illinois: Richard D. Irwin, 1977.

Zaks, Rodnay. *Introduction to Pascal, Including UCSD Pascal.* Berkeley: Sybex, 1980.

Index

Note: Reserved words are in **boldface** type; in addition, reserved words from languages other than BASIC (i.e., Pascal, FORTRAN, or COBOL) are so identified.

The SYBEX Library

YOUR FIRST COMPUTER
by **Rodnay Zaks**   264 pp., 150 illustr., Ref. 0-045
The most popular introduction to small computers and their peripherals: what they do and how to buy one.

DON'T (or How to Care for Your Computer)
by **Rodnay Zaks**   222 pp., 100 illustr., Ref. 0-065
The correct way to handle and care for all elements of a computer system, including what to do when something doesn't work.

INTERNATIONAL MICROCOMPUTER DICTIONARY
140 pp., Ref. 0-067
All the definitions and acronyms of microcomputer jargon defined in a handy pocket-size edition. Includes translations of the most popular terms into ten languages.

FROM CHIPS TO SYSTEMS:
AN INTRODUCTION TO MICROPROCESSORS
by **Rodnay Zaks**   558 pp., 400 illustr. Ref. 0-063
A simple and comprehensive introduction to microprocessors from both a hardware and software standpoint: what they are, how they operate, how to assemble them into a complete system.

INTRODUCTION TO WORD PROCESSING
by **Hal Glatzer**   216 pp., 140 illustr., Ref. 0-076
Explains in plain language what a word processor can do, how it improves productivity, how to use a word processor and how to buy one wisely.

INTRODUCTION TO WORDSTAR™
by **Arthur Naiman**   208 pp., 30 illustr., Ref. 0-077
Makes it easy to learn how to use WordStar, a powerful word processing program for personal computers.

DOING BUSINESS WITH VISICALC®
by **Stanley R. Trost**   200 pp., Ref. 0-086
Presents accounting and management planning applications—from financial statements to master budgets; from pricing models to investment strategies.

EXECUTIVE PLANNING WITH BASIC
by **X. T. Bui**   192 pp., 19 illustr., Ref. 0-083
An important collection of business management decision models in BASIC, including Inventory Management (EOQ), Critical Path Analysis and PERT, Financial Ratio Analysis, Portfolio Management, and much more.

BASIC FOR BUSINESS
by **Douglas Hergert**   250 pp., 15 illustr., Ref. 0-080
A logically organized, no-nonsense introduction to BASIC programming for business applications. Includes many fully-explained accounting programs, and shows you how to write them.

FIFTY BASIC EXERCISES
by J. P. Lamoitier   236 pp., 90 illustr., Ref. 0-056
Teaches BASIC by actual practice, using graduated exercises drawn from everyday applications. All programs written in Microsoft BASIC.

BASIC EXERCISES FOR THE APPLE
by J. P. Lamoitier   230 pp., 90 illustr., Ref. 0-084
This book is an Apple version of *Fifty BASIC Exercises.*

BASIC EXERCISES FOR THE IBM PERSONAL COMPUTER
by J. P. Lamoitier   232 pp., 90 illustr., Ref. 0-088
This book is an IBM version of *Fifty BASIC Exercises.*

INSIDE BASIC GAMES
by Richard Mateosian   352 pp., 120 illustr., Ref. 0-055
Teaches interactive BASIC programming through games. Games are written in Microsoft BASIC and can run on the TRS-80, Apple II and PET/CBM.

THE PASCAL HANDBOOK
by Jacques Tiberghien   492 pp., 270 illustr., Ref. 0-053
A dictionary of the Pascal language, defining every reserved word, operator, procedure and function found in all major versions of Pascal.

INTRODUCTION TO PASCAL (Including UCSD Pascal™)
by Rodnay Zaks   422 pp., 130 illustr. Ref. 0-066
A step-by-step introduction for anyone wanting to learn the Pascal language. Describes UCSD and Standard Pascals. No technical background is assumed.

APPLE® PASCAL GAMES
by Douglas Hergert and Joseph T. Kalash   376 pp., 40 illustr., Ref. 0-074
A collection of the most popular computer games in Pascal, challenging the reader not only to play but to investigate how games are implemented on the computer.

CELESTIAL BASIC: Astronomy on Your Computer
by Eric Burgess   312 pp., 65 illustr., Ref. 0-087
A collection of BASIC programs that rapidly complete the chores of typical astronomical computations. It's like having a planetarium in your own home! Displays apparent movement of stars, planets and meteor showers.

PASCAL PROGRAMS FOR SCIENTISTS AND ENGINEERS
by Alan R. Miller   378 pp., 120 illustr., Ref. 0-058
A comprehensive collection of frequently used algorithms for scientific and technical applications, programmed in Pascal. Includes such programs as curve-fitting, integrals and statistical techniques.

BASIC PROGRAMS FOR SCIENTISTS AND ENGINEERS
by Alan R. Miller   326 pp., 120 illustr., Ref. 0-073
This second book in the ''Programs for Scientists and Engineers'' series provides a library of problem-solving programs while developing proficiency in BASIC.

FORTRAN PROGRAMS FOR SCIENTISTS AND ENGINEERS
by Alan R. Miller   320 pp., 120 illustr., Ref. 0-082
Third in the ''Programs for Scientists and Engineers'' series. Specific scientific and engineering application programs written in FORTRAN.

PROGRAMMING THE 6809
by Rodnay Zaks and William Labiak   520 pp., 150 illustr., Ref. 0-078
This book explains how to program the 6809 in assembly language. No prior programming knowledge required.

PROGRAMMING THE 6502
by Rodnay Zaks   388 pp., 160 illustr., Ref. 0-046
Assembly language programming for the 6502, from basic concepts to advanced data structures.

6502 APPLICATIONS
by Rodnay Zaks   286 pp., 200 illustr., Ref. 0-015
Real-life application techniques: the input/output book for the 6502.

ADVANCED 6502 PROGRAMMING
by Rodnay Zaks   292 pp., 140 illustr., Ref. 0-089
Third in the 6502 series. Teaches more advanced programming techniques, using games as a framework for learning.

PROGRAMMING THE Z80
by Rodnay Zaks   626 pp., 200 illustr., Ref. 0-069
A complete course in programming the Z80 microprocessor and a thorough introduction to assembly language.

PROGRAMMING THE Z8000
by Richard Mateosian   300 pp., 124 illustr., Ref. 0-032
How to program the Z8000 16-bit microprocessor. Includes a description of the architecture and function of the Z8000 and its family of support chips.

THE CP/M® HANDBOOK (with MP/M™)
by Rodnay Zaks   324 pp., 100 illustr., Ref. 0-048
An indispensable reference and guide to CP/M—the most widely-used operating system for small computers.

MASTERING CP/M®
by Alan R. Miller   320 pp., Ref. 0-068
For advanced CP/M users or systems programmers who want maximum use of the CP/M operating system . . . takes up where our *CP/M Handbook* leaves off.

INTRODUCTION TO THE UCSD p-SYSTEM™
by Charles W. Grant and Jon Butah   250 pp., 10 illustr., Ref. 0-061
A simple, clear introduction to the UCSD Pascal Operating System; for beginners through experienced programmers.

A MICROPROGRAMMED APL IMPLEMENTATION
by Rodnay Zaks   350 pp., Ref. 0-005
An expert-level text presenting the complete conceptual analysis and design of an APL interpreter, and actual listing of the microcode.

THE APPLE CONNECTION
by James W. Coffron   228 pp., 120 illustr., Ref. 0-085
Teaches elementary interfacing and BASIC programming of the Apple for connection to external devices and household appliances.

MICROPROCESSOR INTERFACING TECHNIQUES
by Rodnay Zaks and Austin Lesea   458 pp., 400 illustr., Ref. 0-029
Complete hardware and software interconnect techniques, including D to A conversion, peripherals, standard buses and troubleshooting.

SELF STUDY COURSES

Recorded live at seminars given by recognized professionals in the microprocessor field.

INTRODUCTORY SHORT COURSES:
Each includes two cassettes plus special coordinated workbook (2½ hours).

S10—INTRODUCTION TO PERSONAL AND BUSINESS COMPUTING
A comprehensive introduction to small computer systems for those planning to use or buy one, including peripherals and pitfalls.

S1—INTRODUCTION TO MICROPROCESSORS
How microprocessors work, including basic concepts, applications, advantages and disadvantages.

S2—PROGRAMMING MICROPROCESSORS
The companion to S1. How to program any standard microprocessor, and how it operates internally. Requires a basic understanding of microprocessors.

S3—DESIGNING A MICROPROCESSOR SYSTEM
Learn how to interconnect a complete system, wire by wire. Techniques discussed are applicable to all standard microprocessors.

INTRODUCTORY COMPREHENSIVE COURSES:
Each includes a 300-500 page seminar book and seven or eight C90 cassettes.

SB1—MICROPROCESSORS
This seminar teaches all aspects of microprocessors: from the operation of an MPU to the complete interconnect of a system. The basic hardware course (12 hours).

SB2—MICROPROCESSOR PROGRAMMING
The basic software course: step by step through all the important aspects of microcomputer programming (10 hours).

ADVANCED COURSES:

Each includes a 300-500 page workbook and three or four C90 cassettes.

SB3—SEVERE ENVIRONMENT/MILITARY MICROPROCESSOR SYSTEMS

Complete discussion of constraints, techniques and systems for severe environmental applications, including Hughes, Raytheon, Actron and other militarized systems (6 hours).

SB5—BIT-SLICE

Learn how to build a complete system with bit slices. Also examines innovative applications of bit slice techniques (6 hours).

SB6—INDUSTRIAL MICROPROCESSOR SYSTEMS

Seminar examines actual industrial hardware and software techniques, components, programs and cost (4½ hours).

SB7—MICROPROCESSOR INTERFACING

Explains how to assemble, interface and interconnect a system (6 hours).

SOFTWARE

BAS 65™ CROSS-ASSEMBLER IN BASIC

8" diskette, Ref. BAS 65
A complete assembler for the 6502, written in standard Microsoft BASIC under CP/M®.

8080 SIMULATORS

Turns any 6502 into an 8080. Two versions are available for APPLE II.

APPLE II cassette, Ref. S6580-APL(T)
APPLE II diskette, Ref. S6580-APL(D)

FOR A COMPLETE CATALOG
OF OUR PUBLICATIONS

U.S.A.
2344 Sixth Street
Berkeley,
California 94710
Tel: (415) 848-8233
Telex: 336311

SYBEX-EUROPE
4 Place Félix-Eboué
75583 Paris Cedex 12
France
Tel: 1/347-30-20
Telex: 211801

SYBEX-VERLAG
Heyestr. 22
4000 Düsseldorf 12
West Germany
Tel: (0211) 287066
Telex: 08 588 163